Brian D. Singer, CFA
Brinson Partners

Kevin Terhaar, CFA
Brinson Partners

W0005985

Economic Foundations of Capital Market Returns

The Research Foundation of
The Institute of Chartered Financial Analysts

Research Foundation Publications

Economic Foundations of
Capital Market Returns

The Institute of Chartered Financial Analysts is a subsidiary of the Association for Investment Management and Research.

ISBN 0-943205-40-9

Printed in the United States of America

September 1997

Mission

The Research Foundation's mission is to identify, fund, and publish research that is relevant to the AIMR Global Body of Knowledge and useful for AIMR member investment practitioners and investors.

The Research Foundation of
The Institute of Chartered Financial Analysts
P.O. Box 3668
Charlottesville, Virginia 22903
U.S.A.
Telephone: 804-980-3655
Fax: 804-963-6826
E-mail: rf@aimr.org
http://www.aimr.org/aimr/research/research.html

Biographies of Authors

Brian D. Singer, CFA, is a senior asset allocation analyst at Brinson Partners, where he is responsible for developing and managing global asset allocation policy and strategy, performance evaluation, and investment analytics. He is also chair of the Brinson Partners Risk Management Committee. Mr. Singer has worked extensively in analysis of foreign exchange markets and development of procedures for managing currency exposures in global investment portfolios. Most recently, he has been involved in research into the issues of global portfolio management and risk modeling. Mr. Singer holds a B.A. from Northwestern University and an M.B.A. from the University of Chicago.

Kevin Terhaar, CFA, is a senior analyst at Brinson Partners, where he is responsible for analysis of asset classes for global and multi-asset portfolios, including stock and bond market valuation modeling, currency valuation, and risk analysis. Prior to joining Brinson Partners, Mr. Terhaar was manager of investments for a trust office, where he was responsible for asset allocation and investment analysis, performance measurement, and evaluation of alternative investments. He holds a B.A. and an M.A. from the University of Virginia.

Contents

Foreword: "Economic Foundations of Capital Market Returns"

We have all heard the famous observation that if you were to lay all the economists in the world end to end, they still would not reach a conclusion. Or perhaps you know the story about the engineer and the economist who were stranded on a desert island. When a box of canned goods washed ashore, the engineer immediately set about finding a practical way to get to the much-needed sustenance. The economist, however, took a different approach: "It's simple," he said. "Let's assume a can opener!" Or, surely, you have heard about the economist and the trader who go for a stroll and see $20 lying on the ground. The economist walks right past the bill, knowing that because markets are efficient, the bill could not really be there, but the trader stops to pick it up and enjoys a free lunch.

As these stories (and many others I was subjected to during my eight years studying economics) indicate, the profession is not without its detractors. Although perhaps not in the same class as lawyers as the target for jokes, economists are nevertheless routinely regarded as being impractical, arcane, and overly verbose. Still, the economics profession appears to be here to stay and, with it, all of us purveyors of the "dismal science." Consequently, we must assume—there's that word again— that economists truly do offer something of substantial value to financial markets, even though the nature of those contributions is not always clear.

So, what does a modern financial analyst really need to know about economic theory? That question is exactly what Brian Singer and Kevin Terhaar attempt to answer in this monograph. Happily, they succeed in providing at least a partial answer. That statement is not damning them with faint praise, for in a discipline as vast and treacherous as this one, even a little progress is notable. In particular, as the monograph's title implies, they focus their efforts on developing the conceptual foundations for how security returns should be determined, evaluated, and forecast. Although not everything that an analyst needs to know, this material is unquestionably a vital part of the tool kit for anyone studying security markets and financial instruments for a living.

The authors chose to divide their work into two chapters—containing theoretical and empirical analyses, respectively—but I suspect the reader might wish to consume it in smaller doses, and the monograph is written in a manner that allows for such subdivision. From the outset, Singer and Terhaar do a wonderful job of breaking down the economic sources of capital market returns. Starting with the real (i.e., inflation-adjusted) risk-free rate as the base for all other security returns, they patiently guide the reader through the often Byzantine and confusing world of marginal rates of consumption substitution, utility functions, and production-possibility frontiers. They then explain the economic underpinnings of both inflation and risk premiums, tying together in the process such diverse tools as the quantity theory of money and the dividend discount model.

Singer and Terhaar next turn their attention to the way an efficient capital market distributes returns across assets of various risk levels, an endeavor that naturally leads them into a discussion of the celebrated capital asset pricing model (CAPM). This discussion is notable in that it views the determination of equilibrium return expectations in a multicurrency framework, an extension that is missed in most traditional treatments of the CAPM. Beyond this fact, I suspect that the reader will find this discussion valuable for the way it is integrated into the preceding, foundational developments. The authors conclude with an empirical examination of long-term historical returns throughout the world. This material, most of which comments directly on the theoretical concepts already described, provides a satisfying conclusion to the research.

Rather than writing their own version of a microeconomic textbook, Singer and Terhaar have taken a fresher and more satisfying approach. Most importantly, although quite well trained theoretically, they are themselves analysts and so bring the sensibility of the end user to the subject. The result is a highly readable (if not always simple) explanation of how and why security markets function. Readers who have endured some of this material before—usually under the threat of a comprehensive final examination—will be pleasantly surprised at how accessible it has become in the ensuing years. First-time readers will have much here to explore and ponder. Whichever group you may belong to, the Research Foundation is pleased to bring this work to your attention.

Keith C. Brown, CFA
Research Director
The Research Foundation of the
Institute of Chartered Financial Analysts

Acknowledgments

During the years of grading Chartered Financial Analyst examinations and working together on AIMR's Candidate Curriculum Committee, we have had the opportunity to work closely with Keith Brown. One of the concerns we expressed to him is that members of the financial community often fail to make a tight connection between the "finance" they practice and the "economic" fundamentals that lie at the foundation of finance. These musings evolved into this monograph. Therefore, we would like, first and foremost, to thank Keith Brown for his enthusiastic support, helpful direction, and beneficial feedback and comments.

We also acknowledge a great debt of gratitude to the prior research and publishings of Jeffery Diermeier, Roger Ibbotson, and Laurence Siegel on this topic. In addition, we are thankful for the direction and teaching of Denis Karnosky during the years. Their work and tutelage provided an important starting point for our thoughts and the evolution of this monograph.

Special thanks go to Seanna Kim, Shunichi Minami, and our many colleagues at Brinson Partners for their assistance in the research underlying this final product.

Finally, we would like to thank the Research Foundation of the Institute of Chartered Financial Analysts for its support and for the contribution that it makes to advancing the investment community.

Brian D. Singer, CFA
Kevin Terhaar, CFA

Introduction

Harry M. Markowitz, Merton H. Miller, and William F. Sharpe earned the 1990 Nobel Prize in Economic Sciences for their contributions to the field of finance. Although their work has had a dramatic impact on the profession and this award has garnered new respect for the field of financial economics, many asset managers fail to draw adequately upon the economic foundations of capital markets.

The world is rife with "forecasts" of capital market returns. Some of these forecasts prove to be timely and accurate; others are incorrect. Regardless of efficacy, the overwhelming majority of these forecasts tend to be without sufficient support. Forecasts based on historical analysis, either as technical analysis or "fundamental" ratio analysis, stand on no firmer ground than the observation that "this is the way things have always been." Although this type of analysis is useful and often necessary, it is not sufficient.

The equity and bond market return forecasts of any of the global brokerage and investment management firms appear to be based on coherent and considered analysis. Aggregated, however, these forecasts would probably not be internally consistent. In many instances, inconsistencies would arise from segregated bottom-up analyses of individual assets and individual markets. Even among top-down firms, however, the division of analysis of global equity, bond, and alternative asset classes is likely to result in inconsistent capital market expectations. The failure of these forecasts to reflect an acceptable level of "macroconsistency" when viewed in the aggregate rather than in isolation reveals the failure of analysts to draw upon a consistent base of economic analysis.

The objective of this monograph is to develop a process for forecasting long-term returns based on a firm economic foundation. We will look not only at what returns are available to the providers of financial capital but also at how these returns are generated among the myriad assets.

Chapter 1 lays the theoretical groundwork for subsequent empirical analysis of long-term capital market returns. Both the theoretical and the empirical explications are addressed in two distinct parts: the economic foundation of long-term returns, and the apportionment of these returns based on an economically sound asset-pricing model.

The theoretical discussion is designed to provide a foundation for assessing the consistency of aggregate capital market forecasts and, more importantly, a framework for making consistent forecasts. The monograph addresses a broad range of theoretical issues, so the development of each is limited in range. Our intention is not, for example, to review the various theoretical inflation processes, which are well documented in academic literature. Rather, our aim is to tie these theoretical concepts into a cohesive whole that applies to capital market valuation.

The process for determining the magnitude of return that is available to the aggregate capital market focuses on that market in much the same manner as one would focus on an individual company. This "company" happens to be a global conglomerate that owns the real and financial assets that constitute the global capital market.

The capital asset pricing model (CAPM) provides the framework for apportioning the aggregate capital market return among financial assets. We restate the model and review some of its primary implications. The unique nature of global capital markets dictates the discussion of CAPM assumptions. In the final theoretical section, we address exchange rates, inflation, the risk-free rate, and cash returns. These variables are important determinants of returns to global portfolios.

Chapter 2 applies the principles laid out in Chapter 1 to forecasting long-term capital market returns. The primary empirical section demonstrates the forecasting process by melding economic and asset-pricing considerations into actual long-term return forecasts. As the definition of the market changes to accommodate observed market segmentation, the theoretical framework is used to provide multiple long-term return forecasts. Selection of the operable forecast among the alternatives involves an assessment of the future integration of capital markets.

Our concern is not with business cycle fluctuations and the associated short-term variability of capital market returns. Rather, our analysis extends across business cycles to the global economy's long-term return-generating potential and the commensurate long-term (or "equilibrium") asset returns.

1. Theoretical Examination of Capital Market Returns

This chapter presents a model of the aggregate return to capital markets. As with other market returns, the aggregate return to capital markets has three components: the economic basis for the real risk-free rate, the inflation premium, and the aggregate global risk premium.

Real Risk-Free Rate

The real risk-free rate is compensation for forgoing current consumption for certain future consumption.[1] The term "risk-free," by definition, implies the absence of uncertainty in the amount of future consumption. In a free economy, the risk-free rate of interest equilibrates the productivity of the economy and society's time preference for consumption. The former involves what the economy makes available; it specifies an opportunity set. The latter involves individual and aggregate choices regarding the use of that opportunity set.

The risk-free rate is the compensation received for parting with capital in anticipation of the certain receipt of a future consumption flow. Our willingness to part with capital depends on our time preferences for consumption and the productivity of the capital we supply. If we prefer to consume now, we will be reluctant to supply capital. If we prefer to consume in the future, then we will be willing to defer consumption and supply capital now in order to increase our future consumption. The more productive our capital, the more our future consumption increases for each unit of forgone current consumption.

Productivity. The opportunity set can be viewed as the economically feasible trade-off between the limited opportunity for current consumption and the also limited opportunity for future consumption. The economy makes available alternative combinations of current and future consumption. Point A on Figure 1 indicates an economy directed solely toward the production of goods for current consumption. At the other end of the spectrum, at Point B, is an economy that completely forgoes the production of goods for current consumption and focuses on producing goods for future consumption.

Any point on or below the curve connecting Points A and B is feasible for this economy. Any amount of current consumption can be postponed and, depending on the productivity of the economy, converted into future consumption. Points inside the line are feasible but represent production at lower levels than the economy is capable of providing. An economy operating at its potential will be on the curved line between Points A and B, the production-possibility frontier.

"Current consumption" connotes the tangible things that society consumes now. Office supplies and food are examples of such goods. These goods are often referred

---

[1]The phrase "future consumption" will be used interchangeably with "certain future consumption." The certain aspect of consumption is implied.

Figure 1.   Trade-Off between Current and Future Consumption

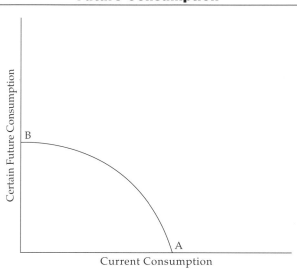

to as nondurable goods. Many goods, however, also provide future consumption. Durable goods, such as a car, provide future service rather than being wholly consumed in the current period. Other durable goods are used in the production of consumption goods. For instance, a battery manufacturer uses not only raw materials, such as lead, but also has long-lived equipment to use in the production process. This long-lived equipment is commonly referred to as "capital equipment," which explicitly recognizes the fact that durable goods provide a stream of future goods or services.

Consider the returns to physical capital—the stream of future consumption that capital provides. There is an implicit trade-off between consuming now and giving up consumption now in order to enhance future consumption. This trade-off defines the rate of substitution of current goods and services that must be forgone for an amount of future goods and services.

Given an economy's current production capabilities and trade-off rate, it could be at any of a number of points along the curve shown in Figure 1. Higher up the curve, the economy would be consuming at a low current level in order to consume a large amount in the future. Because of the limitations of technology, forgoing more current consumption yields diminishing amounts of future consumption. Thus, the slope of a line tangent to the production curve flattens as additional current consumption is traded for future consumption.

The slope of this tangent line is shown in Figure 2. The trade-off between the present and the future is the (marginal) rate of substitution between current and future consumption. The steeper the tangent line, the higher the marginal rate of substitution. Because the slope of the line gives the rate of substitution between the present and the future, it can also be thought of as a return—the additional consumption gained in the future by forgoing consumption today.

For a variety of reasons beyond the scope of this discussion, different economies reflect different levels of productivity. Differing productivity levels affect marginal rates of substitution and returns. Figure 3 shows the production-possibility frontiers for three different economies. All three are assumed to have the ability to consume similar amounts currently.

©The Research Foundation of the ICFA

Figure 2. Marginal Rate of Substitution between Current and Future Consumption

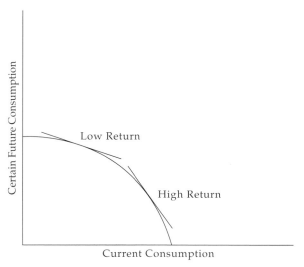

The center curve shows an economy with moderate productivity. The economy inside this curve receives much less future consumption for each unit of current consumption given up; it is less productive than the other two in converting current goods to future goods. Given a fixed amount of forgone current consumption, the less productive economy will have a lower return (marginal rate of substitution) than the other two economies. A more productive economy, shown by the curve farthest out, is able to convert the amount of goods forgone for current consumption into a greater amount of goods for future consumption than can the other economies.

Individuals must allocate their consumption between current and future goods and services. Although we would like unlimited amounts of both, the scarcity of resources limits our ability to consume both now and in the future. Despite that

Figure 3. Production-Possibility Frontiers

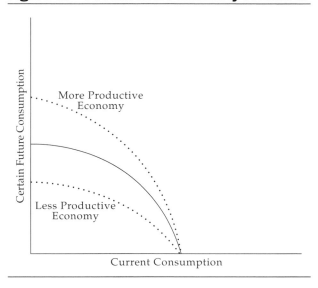

resource constraint, however, we can substitute between current and future consumption. How does society determine how much current consumption to defer in order to consume in the future? The answer depends on the trade-off made available by capital and on the willingness of society's members to make the trade-off.

Time Preference. Each of the three curves in Figure 4 represents constant amounts of satisfaction, which economists refer to as utility. Along any one of these curves, an individual is indifferent to the various combinations of current and future consumption. For example, at Points A and B, the individual would be indifferent between current and future consumption. As current consumption is reduced, ever greater amounts of future consumption are needed to leave the individual as well off.

Although we may be indifferent to any combination of consumption along a single constant utility curve, we prefer more utility to less utility. If we move vertically up from Point A, we increase future consumption at the same level of current consumption. Because we prefer higher levels of consumption, such a shift provides higher utility. Similarly, if we move from Point B to Point D, we increase current consumption at the same level of future consumption. Again, this shift provides a higher level of utility.

Constant utility curves vary with individual preferences. For example, as Figure 5 illustrates, someone who prefers relatively more current consumption will be represented by relatively steep constant utility curves. That individual will require a significant additional amount of future consumption for a decrease in current consumption. Someone who prefers relatively more future consumption will be depicted by a flatter curve and will require only a small increase in future consumption for a decrease in current consumption.

An individual who prefers relatively more current consumption has a high marginal rate of substitution between current and future income. That individual requires a high return from saving and investing in order to forgo consuming now. Conversely, the individual who prefers relatively more future consumption requires a relatively low return, reflecting a low marginal rate of substitution between current and future consumption. Thus, high returns reflect a high rate of substitution between current

Figure 4. Constant Utility Curves

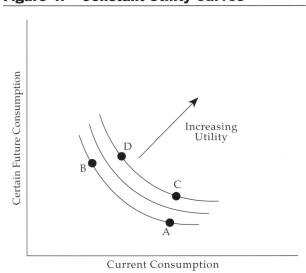

Figure 5. Individual Constant Utility Curves

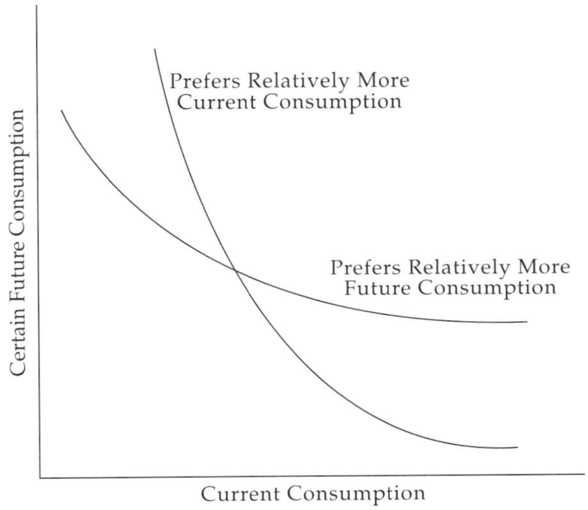

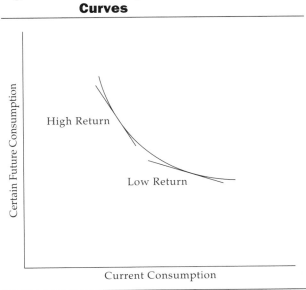

and future consumption. In Figure 6, these high returns are reflected as steep lines. Low returns, reflecting low rates of substitution, are depicted as shallowly sloped lines.

Determination of the Real Risk-Free Rate. The concepts of the opportunity set and the constant utility curve can be combined to determine the equilibrium marginal rate of substitution between current consumption and certain future consumption. In Figure 7, Tangent A of the economywide opportunity set and the economywide constant utility curve indicates the levels of current and future consumption for the economy. More importantly, the slope of the tangent indicates the marginal rate at which current consumption is translated into certain future consumption. This rate is the real risk-free rate.

Figure 6. Economywide Constant Utility Curves

Figure 7. Composition of the Real Risk-Free Rate

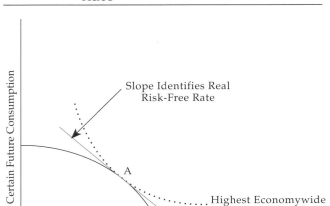

We can form opinions about whether the real risk-free rate is or should be high or low by analyzing societal consumption time preferences and studying the economy's productivity. Japan in the 1970s and 1980s, for example, could be characterized as having a large percentage of its population in the working and saving range and a small percentage in the older, consuming-age range. As such, the Japanese could be characterized as having a relatively shallow constant utility curve.[2] Point A on Figure 8 represents this environment and suggests that across business and credit cycles, the real risk-free rate should be relatively low.

Figure 8. Comparison of Real Risk-Free Rates: Japan

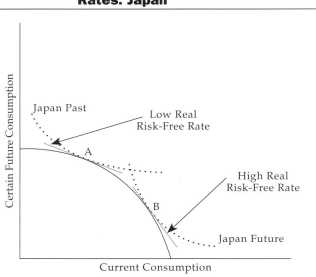

---

[2]Of course, in addition to the demographic factors, social conventions and economic structures may encourage or enforce high savings rates.

Current and future demographic trends in Japan are leading to a shift toward a more consumption-oriented population of older individuals. As the Japanese population ages, the constant utility curve that is tangent to the economywide opportunity set becomes relatively steep, suggesting a higher real risk-free rate. During the transition to that point in time when older individuals dominate the Japanese population, the real risk-free rate is expected to rise and fall in response to other short- and long-term factors. Nonetheless, the demographic pressure will be toward a higher real risk-free rate.

A society's set of constant utility curves provides an interesting comparison among countries with varying levels of productivity. Figure 9 depicts constant utility curves tangent to each of three production-possibility frontiers. According to this figure, the most productive economy could enjoy greater consumption in both the present and the future. The least productive economy is likely to have lower consumption in both periods. Therefore, more-productive economies tend to be wealthier.

In summary, an economy's real risk-free rate of return to capital will depend on both productivity and society's time preference. Changes in productivity or preferences will change the long-run return the economy generates.

The Inflation Premium

The inflation premium is compensation for the depreciation of invested principal because of expected price inflation. This depreciation of a fixed nominal investment reduces certain future consumption. The aggregate return that an economy provides must include a premium that is intended to compensate for any decline in purchasing power because of inflation. The inflation premium, however, does not include any addition for the uncertainty of the inflation estimate; it is only the point estimate of inflation over a period of time.

Actual Inflation. Economists have a bevy of explanations for changes in prices and inflation. Among these are changes in wages, changes in commodity prices, the political party in power, and so forth. These factors may be useful in understanding

Figure 9. Constant Utility Curves and Production-Possibility Frontiers

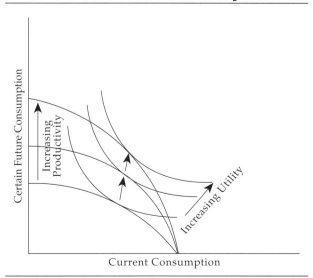

short-term ups and downs in price measures as commonly reported, but in the long run, inflation is a monetary phenomenon. Changes in the money supply and, to a lesser degree, money demand lead to changes in the price level. This theory, the quantity theory of money, hypothesizes that changes in the money supply lead to proportional changes in the price level.

The quantity theory is easy to understand if we view nominal gross domestic product (GDP) from two different angles. On the one hand, GDP is equal to the nominal value of the economy's final output: the average price, P, times Q, the quantity of real output. GDP also can be viewed as the money supply, M, times the number of times the money turns over—that is, the average number of times each dollar is used to buy final output, or the velocity of money, V. Thus,

$$MV = PQ.$$

In terms of rates of change,

$$\%\Delta M + \%\Delta V = \%\Delta P + \%\Delta Q.$$

In the long run, if velocity is relatively stable ($\%\Delta V = 0$) and the quantity of real output is not affected by the money supply, then a change in the money supply leads to a proportional change in the general price level. Figure 10 traces the behavior of velocity in the United States since 1959 based on quarterly nominal GDP and the M1 money supply.[3]

Figure 10. Money Velocity and Interest Rates, 1959–96

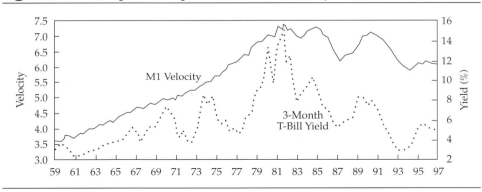

From the start of the 1960s to the beginning of the 1980s, velocity had a distinct upward trend. Two factors explain much of this behavior. First, interest rates also had an upward trend. Because M1 comprises cash and non-interest-bearing checking accounts, the nominal interest rate represents the opportunity cost of holding M1 balances. As interest rates rose, firms and individuals had an incentive to minimize their M1 holdings. Thus, they turned their money over more often and velocity rose. Second, advances in banking and financial technology during the 1960s and 1970s (such as the growth of money-market mutual funds) allowed reductions in checking balances relative to the dollar amount of transactions.

Although velocity tended to rise during the 1960–80 period, it did not grow without

---

[3]M1 is defined as cash plus checking balances. This definition essentially includes only the most liquid instruments and those generally used in transactions. Although credit cards are used widely, those balances are not considered money because they are debts rather than assets. Also, in the United States, M1 is adjusted for balances swept overnight into interest-bearing (and non-M1) money measures. These "sweep-adjusted" data are available from the Cleveland Federal Reserve.

bound, nor did it fall to zero after the 1980s. Indeed, since the early 1980s, it has fluctuated between 6.0 and 7.5, depending on interest rates.

In the short run, unanticipated changes in the money supply can affect the real economy by causing misallocation of resources, thus contributing to business cycle fluctuations. Moreover, velocity can be quite unstable, especially outside the United States. As a result, blind adherence to the quantity theory is ill advised, but the concept still has important implications for long-term inflation analysis. We will make use of the quantity theory in forming long-term inflation premium forecasts.

Figure 11 plots year-over-year consumer price inflation in the United States (based on the U.S. Consumer Price Index, CPI) since 1960 and the year-over-year growth rate in M1 lagged two years (changes in the money supply tend to lead inflation by roughly two years). Money supply growth is what allowed the two 1970s' oil shocks to evolve into generalized inflation rather than a rise in the price of energy relative to the prices of other goods. One might argue that the 1970s' oil shocks are evidence that inflation can occur for reasons other than monetary stimulus. In fact, the oil shocks are perhaps the best proof of the validity of the quantity theory of money. The first oil shock caught nearly all countries off guard. Viewed in isolation, the rise in the price of oil is seen strictly as a rise relative to other prices. No generalized increase in the price level would necessarily have occurred. In an attempt to keep their economies from being adversely affected by the oil price increase, central banks around the world began printing money and allowing the general price level to rise with the rise in oil prices.

Broad long-term trends in inflation tend to be patterned after broad long-term trends in money supply growth. Recent M1 growth has been more loosely correlated with inflation than previously. Because of financial innovations and the resultant lower holdings of M1 for transactions, M1 has a somewhat weaker effect on prices. Nonetheless, if the Federal Reserve were to supply substantially more money than the public desired to hold, the result would be a general increase in the price level.

Figure 12 shows that Japan, a country generally noted for its low inflation, witnessed year-over-year inflation (Japan's CPI) in excess of 30 percent at the time of the first oil shock. By the second oil shock, however, Japan and some other countries (regrettably, not the United States) had learned their lessons and did not accommodate the oil price increase. Although inflation soared in the United Kingdom and the United States, it remained low in Japan, despite Japan's complete dependence on oil imports. In Japan, oil-related prices rose and non-oil-related prices compensated, leaving the general rate of price inflation roughly the same as before the shock.

Figure 11. U.S. Money Supply Growth and Inflation, 1959–96

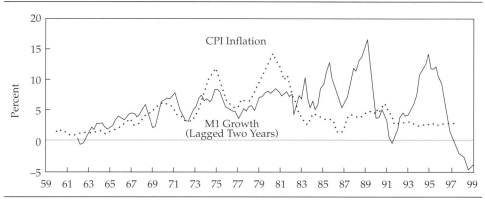

Figure 12. Japanese Money Supply Growth and Inflation, 1971–96

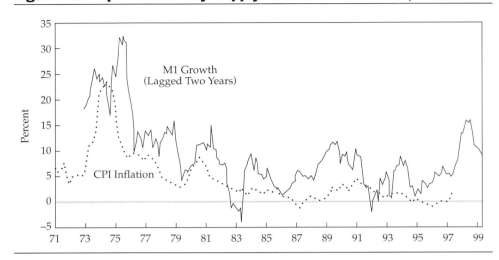

The U.K. experience (inflation based on the U.K. CPI) is traced in Figure 13.[4] As in the United States, the second oil shock caused a spike in consumer price inflation, although not as great as during the first shock. Even aside from the oil shocks, higher money growth in the 1970s was associated with higher inflation. When the growth of the money supply was curtailed, inflation responded (with a lag). The low current rates of growth in the money supply are consistent with inflation remaining relatively low since the mid-1980s.

Figure 13. U.K. Money Supply Growth and Inflation, 1971–96

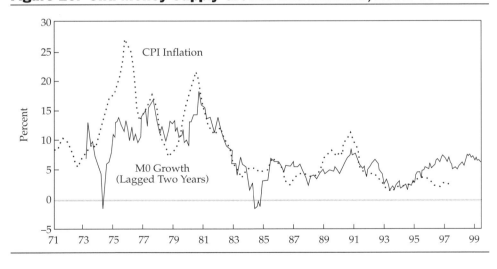

The validity of the quantity theory can be reinforced by examining the relationship between inflation and the money supply among countries. Figure 14 plots the observed annual rate of inflation for selected countries against the annual rate of money supply growth. The strong positive long-term relationship is indicated by the high correlation,

---

[4]For many years, the Bank of England did not publish a money series strictly comparable to M1. The closest available series is M0, which is narrower because it primarily captures notes and coin but not noninterest transactions balances. For the sake of consistency across countries and continuity of data series, we have chosen to use M0 rather than "higher" money definitions, such as M2 or M4, in our analysis.

Figure 14. Money Supply Growth and Inflation: Selected Countries, June 30, 1973–September 30, 1996

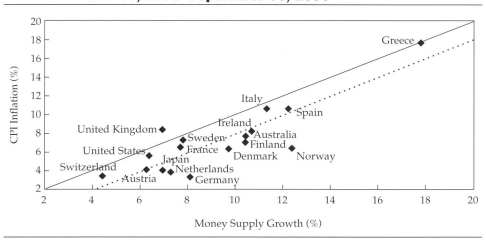

0.86.[5] If there had been a perfect one-to-one correspondence between the money supply growth rate and the rate of inflation, then all points would have lain on the diagonal.

Although the relationship between inflation and M1 is not exact, most of the inflation data points fall on or below the money supply line. The quantity theory of money framework can help explain this phenomenon. An increase in the money supply must result in an increase in prices unless real output increases or velocity falls. As Figure 14 indicates, for most countries, the money supply grew at a faster rate than prices. In fact, the difference between the dotted line and the solid diagonal would correspond with the real GDP expansion among these countries of about 2.0 percent to 2.5 percent annually.[6] Because prices rose by about 2.1 percent less than money supply growth, velocity over the full period did not change systematically.

Time-series data provide evidence similar to that of the cross-sectional data. From the first oil shock, the general tendency has been for central banks to pursue less-stimulative and less-variable monetary policies. The result has been declining rates of inflation. Figure 15 shows year-over-year aggregate money supply growth and inflation averaged for Canada, Germany, Japan, the United Kingdom, and the United States. It demonstrates the broad relationship between money supply growth and inflation over time. The relationship is stronger in some countries—notably in Japan and the United Kingdom—and weaker in others—the United States is a prime example.

Because recent years have been characterized by a lack of supply shocks, central banks have been able to behave in a noninflationary manner. Despite the absence of severe macroeconomic pressures recently, the trend toward more-stable and less-inflationary monetary policies is likely to continue.

Inflationary Expectations. Inflation and inflationary expectations are not necessarily created in the same ways. Long-term inflationary expectations require long-term forecasts of money supply growth. Those forecasts are extremely difficult to make, because central bank objectives change over time. Understanding the process

---

[5]Dropping the one high-inflation/high-money-supply-growth point from the chart reduces the correlation, but only to 0.79—still relatively strong.

[6]The dotted line was constructed to be parallel to the diagonal but plotted through the average intercept of the data points. In other words, this construction is similar to a regression with the beta forced to be 1.0.

Figure 15. Money Supply Growth and Inflation: Average for Canada, Germany, Japan, United Kingdom, and United States, 1970–96

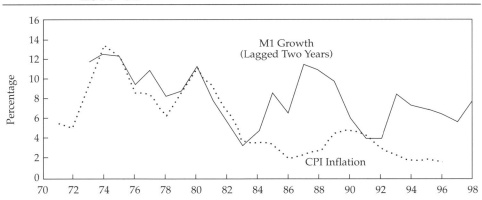

by which central banks set monetary policy provides a major leap forward. One means of understanding this process is by gauging the independence of the central bank. The independence of the central bank from the financing apparatus of government is crucial. A lack of independence implies that the government can turn to inflationary money creation to finance a budget deficit rather than issuing bonds.

Alesina and Summers (1993) derived a measure of central bank independence based on two related measures: political independence and economic independence. They defined political independence as "the ability of the central bank to select its policy objectives without influence from the government." This ability involves consideration of board appointments, length of appointments, whether government representatives sit on the board, and whether government approval of monetary policy is required. Independence also depends on whether "price stability" is an explicitly stated central bank objective. Economic independence is based on the central bank's ability to use instruments of monetary policy without restrictions. The most common restriction is the extent to which the central bank is required to finance government deficits.

Figure 16 illustrates the relationship between inflation and an index of central bank independence derived by Alesina and Summers. A high index number indicates a relatively independent central bank, and a low number, the converse. The correlation between long-term inflation and the index is –0.79. According to the figure, the more independent a central bank, the lower a country's inflation rate. This relationship is a powerful tool for forecasting inflation. As central banks become more (less) independent, we would likely expect a decrease (increase) in the rate of price inflation. Although the process may take some time to evolve, long-term inflation expectations can be directed in an appropriate manner.

The behavior of the participants in the economy is equally important in determining the central bank's behavior. If the central bank can pursue real economic goals, rather than focus exclusively on the price level, then the temptation to abandon price stability in favor of lower unemployment and greater output may become too great. Whether central banks succumb to this temptation depends on how people and firms in the economy react to the central bank's signals.

Two major hypotheses regarding the formation of inflation expectations are the adaptive and the rational expectations hypotheses. The adaptive expectations theory hypothesizes that inflation expectations are formed on the basis of past and current inflation realizations. If inflation has been high, then inflation expectations generally

Figure 16. Inflation and Central Bank Independence, 1957–95

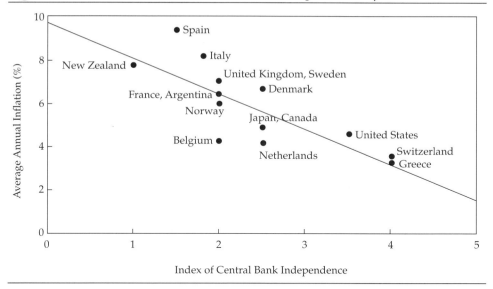

will be high. If inflation has been low, then the expectation will be for future inflation also to be low. Although this hypothesis does not seem rigorous, it is well grounded in empirical observation.

Figure 17 shows actual year-over-year inflation and one-year-forward inflationary expectations since 1971, according to the *Survey of Professional Forecasters,* compiled by the Federal Reserve Bank of Philadelphia. The pattern of expected inflation indicates that forecasters predicted that inflation for the next four quarters would look much like the inflation rate they were experiencing at the time the forecasts were made. Predicted inflation lags actual inflation by a year or so, suggesting that forecasters were generally caught off guard by shifts in the inflation rate and were slow to catch up to the new trends.

Figure 17. Actual and Expected Inflation, 1971–96

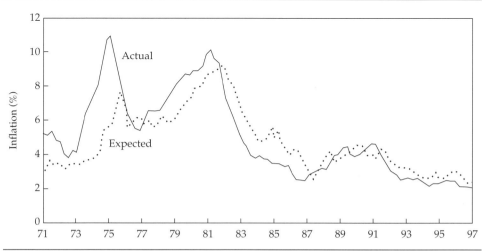

Source: Based on data from the *Survey of Professional Forecasters,* compiled by the Federal Reserve Bank of Philadelphia.

An alternative basic premise of the rational expectations hypothesis is that you cannot fool all the people all the time. Where central banks are not independent of government control, the money supply is often used as a tool for purposes associated with short-term real economic considerations or even narrow political objectives. To increase output and cut unemployment during a recession, the government might increase the rate of growth of the money supply. Initially, the looser monetary policy may have the intended effect. If people form expectations adaptively, the central bank can pursue a policy of ever more expansionary monetary policy. The public is continually fooled into thinking that price increases signal higher relative prices for the goods or labor they supply. Each adjustment in the public's inflation expectations, however, is one step behind the monetary authority's increasingly inflationary monetary policy. When workers are offered higher wages, they think the offer signals increased real wages, so the amount of labor supplied increases. A business, in the face of rising prices for the goods it sells, also takes these increases to be real. It increases production and sales accordingly. Output growth remains strong and unemployment stays low—at the cost of ever-increasing inflation.

In contrast, when expectations are formed rationally, people catch on to this change in policy. They eventually see that the price increases are, in fact, a generalized inflation process. Because people's expectations adjust, the central bank can surprise them only temporarily with an inflation rate greater than anticipated. With rational expectations, the rapid inflation delivers lower unemployment and greater output only temporarily. Empirical observation of hyperinflationary economies lends credence to the rational expectations view, in that increasingly expansionary monetary policies have proved to be ultimately unsustainable.

An equilibrium in which inflation surprises in the same direction continually fool people is difficult to accept. Over short-to-intermediate periods of time, however, expectations appear to be formed adaptively (it can be rational to assume that the best unbiased forecast of a variable is its current value). In the long run, people are rational and responsive to changes in the environment.

In making inflation forecasts, therefore, we must decide how willing we are to accept that central banks have forsworn inflation surprise as a tool to boost the real economy. Using the history of the 1970s and 1980s as a guide, governments seem to have learned their lesson and are now less apt to pressure their central banks to engage in short-run stimuli at the cost of long-term damage to reputation.

The Risk Premium

The aggregate global risk premium is compensation for the *uncertainty* associated with the future consumption an investment makes available. The source of this uncertainty may be in levels of cash flows from the investment or in the risk that inflation will differ from the anticipated level. The risk premium is the expected reward for assuming uncertainty in the future value of an investment. Our model of the long-term aggregate capital market risk premium is not based on historical or adjusted historical capital market performance but on the underlying base of economic activity. Rather than simply extrapolating the past, the objective is understanding the source of the risk premium. By understanding the source of this premium, we should be able to make more-educated estimates of its magnitude.

Every business decision involves determining how to expend scarce resources in an attempt to maximize wealth. Given a choice between investing in a project that provides a stream of certain future consumption and another project that has the same expected consumption stream, any rational individual will choose the project that provides certain future consumption. To undertake projects with uncertain cash flows, investors must be provided with relatively high expected returns. Risk is a function of the uncertainty associated with the future consumption that an investment makes available. The greater the risk, the greater must be the expected return. The portion of the return that provides compensation for risk is called the risk premium.

The aggregate risk premium investors expect from all capital goods acquired is an amalgam of the risk premiums that each investor expects of each individual investment decision. Consequently, the aggregate return the economy makes available to investors is determined by the projects investors undertake. The combined uncertainty associated with these investments is identical to the uncertainty associated with the future consumption the aggregate economy makes available.

The risk premium model we present is based upon the premise that an asset's value is equal to the present value of the future income stream it provides. A real asset is defined as any source of future income flows, and a financial asset is defined as any claim on a real asset. The income represents the potential for future consumption. With a given real risk-free return and a known inflation premium, an asset's risk premium accounts for the uncertainty that the income stream will provide a level of consumption different from the level expected at the time the asset is purchased. The risk premium estimate is obtained by subtracting the real risk-free rate and the inflation premium from the return the income stream represents.

An asset's value is the sum of the discounted values of all future cash flows. Various cash flow discounting models have been derived based on cash flow growth and discount rate assumptions. The simplest method, and the one that requires the most restrictive assumptions, is the constant-growth model. Using a constant discount rate, the constant-growth model discounts future cash flows, which are assumed to grow at a constant rate period after period.

The present value of a set of cash flows, V_0, that grows at a constant rate, g, beginning with an expected cash flow at the end of the first period, C_1, and discounted at a constant periodic rate, r, can be determined with the following simplified equation:[7]

$$V_0 = \frac{C_1}{(r-g)}.$$ (1)

Thus, an asset with an expected cash flow in one year of \$1, annual cash flow growth of 6 percent, and an annual discount rate of 10 percent is valued at \$25.

$$V_0 = \frac{\$1}{(0.10-0.06)} = \$25.$$

In this model, the annual discount rate applied to the cash flows is 10 percent. This discount rate can be turned around and also thought of as a return. For instance, an asset priced at \$25 with an initial payment of \$1 at the end of the first year and future year-end payments growing at the rate of 6 percent would have an annual return of 10 percent. So, the discount rate and expected return to the investor are equivalent when the asset's price is the same as the valuation obtained from the model.

The model can be applied to value individual assets or to value an aggregation of assets.[8] An important aggregation in exploring the economic basis for capital market

---

[7]This formulation is the standard Gordon–Shapiro model as specified in Gordon and Shapiro (1956).

[8]This discussion benefits from the earlier work of Diermeier, Ibbotson, and Siegel (1984) and Diermeier (1990).

returns is a society's assets. Societal wealth is equal to the sum of present consumption and the present value of all future consumption (the income stream). Using the constant-growth model, societal wealth, W_s, is equal to current consumption, I_0, plus the present value of all real assets. The present value of all real assets can be estimated with the constant-growth model, assuming an income stream of I_1, which begins one year hence of I_1, grows at the constant annual rate of G, and is discounted at a constant annual rate of R; that is,

$$W_S = I_0 + \frac{I_1}{(R-G)}. \tag{2}$$

The income, I_1, accrues to the factors of production, which we aggregate into two broad categories—human capital, or labor, and physical capital, or property, plant, and equipment. More precisely, the income stream produced by society's economic activity accrues to the providers of labor as wages, providers of property as rent, and providers of plant and equipment as investment returns. We have consolidated property, plant, and equipment into a single category because ownership of these real assets is generally consolidated within financial capital—stocks and bonds—and we are ultimately interested in the returns to these financial assets—the ownership claims on real assets.

Societal income, I_1, can be divided into the income that accrues to the providers of human capital, I_L, and to the providers of financial capital, I_K. Thus,

$$I_1 = I_L + I_K. \tag{3}$$

From Equation 3, the growth of societal income is equal to the sum of the change in labor income plus the change in income to capital; that is,

$$\Delta I = \Delta I_L + \Delta I_K.$$

Dividing both sides by I_1 yields the percentage change, or growth rate, in societal income. In addition, we can multiply the right-hand side by ratios equaling 1 to get the following:

$$\frac{\Delta I}{I_1} = \frac{\Delta I_L}{I_L}\frac{I_L}{I_1} + \frac{\Delta I_K}{I_K}\frac{I_K}{I_1}.$$

Rewriting this equation in terms of weights and growth rates, we get the growth rate of societal income, G, equal to the weighted growth rates of labor's income, G_L, and financial capital's income, G_K; thus,

$$G = S_L G_L + S_K G_K, \tag{4}$$

where the terms S_L and S_K denote the income shares of labor and capital, respectively.

If labor's share of income, S_L, is constant, then the growth rates of income accruing to labor, G_L, and financial capital, G_K, must be equal and identical to the growth rate of societal income, G. If these growth rates were not equal, we would observe drift in the income shares. For instance, if the growth in income accruing to capital were greater than the growth in income accruing to labor, eventually capital's share of income would approach 100 percent and labor's would approach zero.

Labor's share of income can be directly observed by evaluating the components of GDP. U.S. national income account information is quite detailed, but outside the United States, the data are sparse, of limited duration, and inconsistently defined.

Mitigating some of these problems, the Organization for Economic Cooperation and Development (OECD) provides country-by-country and aggregate national income account statistics. Although the OECD goes to great lengths to report comparable data, the degree of detail is significantly diminished. Using the OECD data, labor's income share is equal to resident producers' employee compensation divided by total income (the sum of producers' employee compensation, fixed-capital compensation, operating surplus, and the statistical discrepancy).

Figure 18 shows labor's income share for the United States and the OECD in aggregate from 1960 through 1995. The U.S. labor share since 1960 has been fairly constant at about 65 percent of total income. The aggregate OECD data also indicate a stable share, but at a slightly lower level, 61 percent.

Figure 18. Share of Labor in National Income: United States and OECD Countries, 1960–95

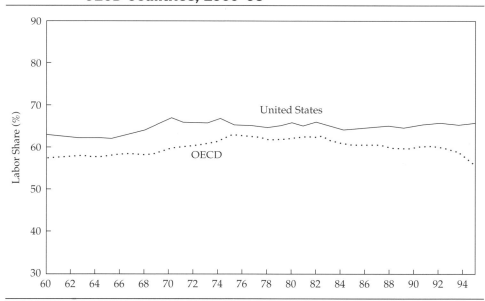

Based on the labor-share data, we assume that the growth rates of income accruing to labor and financial capital equal aggregate societal income growth. Therefore, societal wealth can be segmented into current consumption and the two constant-growth components—one for labor, W_L, and one for providers of financial capital, W_K—with the assumption that income growth for both components is equal to the societal income growth rate, G. Substituting Equation 3 into Equation 2 produces

$$W_s = I_0 + \frac{I_L}{(R-G)} + \frac{I_K}{(R-G)}. \tag{5}$$

As for the capital market component, the value of aggregate wealth represented by capital markets can be estimated to equal the present value of an income stream that begins at the end of Year 1 at I_K and grows at a constant rate equal to the rate of growth of societal income, G:

$$W_K = \frac{I_K}{(R-G)}. \tag{6}$$

By rearranging terms, the discount rate, R, is equal to the first year's income accruing to financial capital as a percentage of wealth represented by the capital market plus the growth rate of income. In nominal terms,

$$R = \frac{I_K}{W_K} + G. \tag{7}$$

Expressing this relationship in real terms merely requires subtracting the inflation rate, $\%\Delta P$, from each side of the equation.[9] Thus,

$$R - \%\Delta P = \frac{I_K}{W_K} + G - \%\Delta P. \tag{8}$$

The real return available to providers of financial capital, R_r, is equal to the first year's income plus the real growth rate of income, G_r, as determined by societal economic activity; that is,[10]

$$R_r = \frac{I_K}{W_K} + G_r. \tag{9}$$

This model can be used to estimate the aggregate real return available to the owners of financial capital, given the first year's equilibrium income and the growth rate of societal income. Both of these variables can be estimated on a forward-looking basis in order to derive a long-term aggregate capital market real return forecast.

The world, however, is never quite as simple as we would like. In addition to compensation in the form of income flows, asset redemptions and buybacks provide cash flows that are identical to income payments in terms of economic substance but are different in form. In aggregate, compensation through the reduction of assets owned is equal but opposite in sign to the net new issuance of securities. As such, any change in capital market wealth, ΔW_K, in one year is equal to the cash income, I_K, during the year less net new issuance, N_1, plus the capital gain attributable to price appreciation, A; that is,

$$\Delta W_K = (I_K - N_1) + A. \tag{10}$$

In percentage terms, the change in wealth relative to total wealth is equal to income less net new issuance as a percent of total wealth plus the appreciation as a percent of total wealth:

$$\frac{\Delta W_K}{W_K} = \frac{(I_K - N_1)}{W_K} + \frac{A}{W_K}. \tag{11}$$

Because $\Delta W_K / W_K$ is simply the aggregate capital market nominal return, R, and A/W_K is the growth rate, G, the aggregate return can be more completely stated as the sum of the first year's income net of net new issuance plus the growth rate. In real terms,

$$R_r = \frac{(I_K - N_1)}{W_K} + G_r. \tag{12}$$

---

[9]We have elected to use simple addition and subtraction through most of this monograph in order to keep the exposition simple. This approach is valid if we are using continuously compounded returns. Alternatively, we could assume that growth rates and returns are geometric but that cross-products are small and safely ignored.

[10]Because we are developing a model of long-run, or equilibrium, returns, the first year's income should be equilibrium (or normalized) income rather than a current rate; the global economy and financial market may not be in equilibrium.

This model provides an economic foundation for forecasting the aggregate long-term real return available to the owners of financial capital. Using the model requires estimates of the first year's equilibrium capital market income and net new issuance of securities relative to the aggregate market capitalization plus an estimate of the long-term real growth rate of societal income.

The real return is available to capital markets to compensate providers of capital for parting with their capital and for uncertainty regarding the future income stream. If the return had been stated in nominal terms, it would simply provide additional compensation for the protection of invested capital against depreciation as a result of inflation. Similarly, the aggregate risk premium can be determined by subtracting the real risk-free rate from the aggregate real return.

The aggregate global market risk premium can be compared with the risk associated with the global market to determine how much compensation investors should receive for incurring risk. The price of risk is simply the ratio of the risk premium to total risk, commonly referred to as the Sharpe ratio. If we assume that, in equilibrium, the price of risk is constant across assets and investors, then we can apply it to various measures of asset risk to determine the risk premium that the assets should afford. The price of risk, within the context of an equilibrium asset-pricing model, enables us to divide the global market risk premium among individual assets.

Although Equation 12 is valid for the market as a whole, not much physical capital is represented as financial capital available to investors. So, a distinction will be made between society's wealth, which receives a return generated by the economywide process, and financial wealth.

Marketable Claims on Real Assets

Once the aggregate real return to capital has been determined according to the framework we have laid out, we can consider how that return gets distributed to the various forms of assets. In equilibrium, all assets should receive the certain, risk-free return. Those assets that provide uncertain future consumption must provide a risk premium in addition. This risk premium gets "distributed" according to the riskiness of different assets. But what are these different assets?

Ultimately, we describe the long-term potential returns that investors receive for holding portfolios of financial assets. What we are starting with, however, is a model of the returns available to society's real assets. We will be able to develop returns to financial assets only if the securities are claims on real assets. Then, the financial assets' returns can be determined by using the aggregate capital market. So, we first identify various types of real assets and then look at financial assets and discuss the validity of their inclusion on the list of claims on the real assets.

Real Assets—Factors of Production. A real asset provides a stream of consumption of real goods or services and is not consumed fully in the production process. Real assets include human capital, real estate, and capital goods.

Human capital. Human capital is the value of the education and knowledge an individual accumulates. The monetary value of an individual's human capital would equal the present discounted value of that person's expected lifetime earnings stream. Human capital gets compensated directly through wages, salaries, and benefits. Thus, labor compensation for human capital is separate from the return to other forms of wealth.

One large problem with human capital should be readily apparent: assigning value to it. Unless claims on human capital exist in some form and their risk characteristics can be determined, there will be no basis for assigning it a return.

Real estate. Real estate assets include all land and structures—commercial, residential, and agricultural property. Clearly, real estate should be counted as part of society's wealth. The compensation to real estate is referred to as rent. Even properties on which rent is not explicit have an implicit return to them; the rent on or return to an owner-occupied house is the service flow the owner receives from living there. Alternatively, the return is measured by the regular payment at which the property could be rented to another party.

Like human capital, the price of much real estate is unobservable. Very few direct claims on this form of wealth exist. Most properties are not regularly priced in a competitive process. Real estate markets are very illiquid and information on properties is limited; the vast majority of properties come onto the market only rarely. At any given time, the number of buyers is small and few properties are for sale.

Capital goods. In producing output, a business uses not only raw materials but also some mixture of people, real estate, and equipment. Along with human capital and real estate, production equipment should also be considered a real asset. Any piece of equipment that is long lived and that is not consumed in the production process, as are raw materials, is a capital good. Just as human capital represents the present value of lifetime earnings, a capital good represents the stream of future output that it can be used to produce. It can also be considered a real asset because its output is equivalent to a return to the capital.

Financial Assets—Claims on Factors of Production. Financial assets represent ownership of real assets. Our focus is the analysis of tradable capital market assets, which are composed of financial assets rather than real assets.

Equities. Generally, people think of claims on capital goods—the means of production—as equities. An equity represents a claim on the residual value of a firm's cash flows after all other claimants (debt holders, employees, suppliers, and the government) have been paid. The equity's value also equals the value of the firm's assets, both tangible and intangible, in excess of its liabilities.

Because a firm's tangible assets include any property and buildings it owns in addition to the capital goods within those buildings, some real estate wealth will be captured in the equity markets. The value of real estate, however, is inseparable from the value of a firm's other assets.

In a similar line of reasoning, the value of a firm could be composed partly of human capital, meaning that human capital is captured to some extent in financial assets. If firms with more human capital have more attractive growth and future cash flow prospects, then they may garner higher valuations than other, similar firms. Ultimately, the increased values will be attributable to the human capital.

Many forms of equity do not have claims available. For instance, homeowners' equity is not generally found among the world's financial assets (equity markets). The value of a house over and above the mortgage debt primarily accrues to the homeowner rather than being securitized. Likewise, many businesses are held privately. Again, these entities represent wealth to society, but the ownership claims are not found in the traded markets.

The market for equities is large. Currently, about 50 countries, from Australia to Zimbabwe, have equity markets. The market value of many equity markets, however, overstates the availability of these claims. For many investors, some markets are partially or almost wholly inaccessible. For example, the legal maximum of foreign ownership of any company in South Korea is 23 percent. This restriction does not necessarily bias the market capitalization; rather, it nullifies the assumption of a globally integrated capital market and means that market capitalizations may not truly represent global investors' investment opportunities.

Other markets exhibit a factor that has the potential of biasing capitalization upward. Extensive cross-holdings among companies, indicated in Table 1, can lead to double counting, which has the effect of boosting the apparent level of wealth and of limiting the availability of shares to outsiders.

Table 1. Percentage of Shares Cross-Held: 22 Equity Markets

Country	Percent Cross-Held
Australia	13.5%
Austria	18.4
Belgium	36.0
Canada	14.6
Denmark	4.2
Finland	11.6
France	25.3
Germany	20.4
Hong Kong	23.3
Ireland	12.7
Italy	23.7
Japan	37.8
Malaysia	14.8
Netherlands	12.7
New Zealand	30.2
Norway	9.8
Singapore	11.4
Spain	21.8
Sweden	18.8
Switzerland	4.2
United Kingdom	6.5
United States	4.5

Sources: Salomon Brothers; International Finance Corporation.

Because of these cross-holdings, equity market capitalizations are adjusted downward. Aggregated at December 31, 1995, market exchange rates, the market values of the world's equity markets available to global investors are $5,721 billion in the U.S. market, $6,289 in the other developed markets, and $1,706 billion in the emerging markets, for a total of $13,716 billion.[11]

Debt. The treatment of debt is not quite as straightforward as it is for equity. Because equity represents the residual claims of owners on firms' assets, it is a form in which real wealth can be held. A large portion of the debt traded in the world, however, has no underlying real wealth.

Corporate debt would certainly represent a claim on net wealth because it is one of the first claims on a firm's real assets. Corporate debt is no different from corporate equity in terms of wealth, except that the debt has a more senior position in the list

---

[11]The market values for the United States and for the other developed equity markets are from Salomon Brothers' Broad Market Index (BMI), adjusted for the level of cross-holdings; this index has more extensive coverage than some other equity indexes. The emerging market capitalizations are from International Finance Corporation data adjusted to exclude our estimate of cross-held shares.

of claimants.[12] Whether other forms of debt represent net wealth to society is not clear. Think about a mortgage-backed security (MBS) for instance. The purchaser of an MBS has a financial asset that pays principal and interest. Consider the other side of the MBS, however. On the paying end are homeowners, meeting their monthly mortgage obligations. In effect, the MBS is simply a vehicle by which mortgage payments can be efficiently transferred from one person to another. The security itself represents an asset to the purchasers and a debt to the borrowers, in equal amounts. Through an MBS, one person's asset is another person's liability; thus, these securities do not represent net wealth to society. They do, however, represent a claim on wealth, insofar as they are claims on a real asset (the real estate asset of the borrower). Therefore, an MBS can be considered a financial claim on wealth.

Through similar reasoning, we can deduce that government bonds do not represent net wealth to society but might represent net claims on wealth. In this case, one person's asset (the bond) is another person's debt (tax liability), and the result is no net gain to society. All that has been achieved is a transfer from taxpayers to bondholders; the bondholders have a claim on the assets of current and future taxpayers. This simplification ignores the fact that the government bonds could, in some sense, represent claims on the real assets of the government: roads, buildings, tanks, planes, and other property and infrastructure. The value of such assets, however, is likely to be small relative to the total market value of the debt outstanding, and unlike corporate debt or MBS, government bonds are not collateralized by those real assets. (Subordinated corporate debentures also may not have specific assets as collateral but do have first claim on the assets of the firm after the senior debtholders have been paid, so their value is backed by wealth.)

Conceptually, a government bond is backed by the word of the government that the principal and interest will be paid when due. Future bond payments are collateralized by the ability of the government to extract revenue from the taxpayers. Because the payments are to be made in the future, they represent taxation of future income, but the value of human capital is the present value of future income. So, if the government can demand, through taxes, part of the stream of future wage income, then by issuing bonds, it has created claims on human capital. In effect, the government can cause involuntary securitization of human capital, adding to net financial claims on wealth, although not to society's true wealth.

Estimates of the dollar value of investable bonds at December 31, 1995, are $9,929 billion for the U.S. debt market, $12,852 billion for other developed markets, $747 billion for the emerging markets, and $327 billion for the high-yield markets, for a total of $23,855 billion.[13]

Cash. Just as with any other fixed-income security, cash represents a claim on wealth. The only difference is that cash is of short duration and bonds are of longer duration. This difference, however, leads to a major distinction in distribution of capital market returns. Because cash assets are of short duration, they do not carry a risk premium; their real return is known with (near) certainty. In equilibrium, all assets receive the real risk-free return plus an inflation premium. Because cash is not compensated with a risk premium, no additional portion of the aggregate return needs to be "distributed" to cash.

---

[12]Obviously, this argument is very simplified along the lines of Modigliani and Miller (1958).

[13]The values for the developed and emerging bond markets are from Salomon Brothers, and the high-yield bond data are from CS First Boston.

Derivatives. Derivatives, including options, futures contracts, and swaps, are not claims on wealth. The reason is quite simple: Derivatives are nothing more than contracts to exchange cash flows. These contracts may have a value, but the value or gain to one party is offset by a loss of equal magnitude by the counterparty. The values themselves can be based on assets, but the contracts cannot represent wealth. If they did, then we could create unlimited wealth by issuing more options or futures contracts.

Distribution of Capital Market Returns

The various financial assets just described earn some portion of the aggregate capital market return. The question now is how that return gets apportioned among these assets. We often hear comments that "stocks will earn 10 percent in the long run" or "bonds are expected to outperform cash by 150 basis points over time," but many of those kinds of *ad hoc* statements have little justification. A fundamentally sound model, rather than extrapolation of history, should help to rationally form return expectations for asset classes.

The Capital Asset Pricing Model. The primary framework used to determine asset returns is the capital asset pricing model (CAPM). We chose the CAPM rather than one of the alternatives, such as APT (arbitrage pricing theory), because the CAPM specifically derives and identifies its risk factor from a fundamental equilibrium framework. Other pricing models generally do not specify *ex ante* which factors are compensated in equilibrium. Therefore, the equilibrium compensation of an asset is not possible to specify uniquely.

One important point about the CAPM is that it is a model for pricing risky assets. The risk-free rate of return (or interest rate) is exogenous. The compensation for an investor taking no risk is given by the real risk-free rate and the inflation premium. The CAPM shows that if investors elect to take risk, they may be compensated in addition to the risk-free rate. Whether they are paid for taking risk depends on the nature of the risk.

CAPM assumptions.[14] The first of the CAPM's eight assumptions is that *all investors construct efficient portfolios*; that is, given their beliefs about assets' expected returns, risks, and correlations, investors form portfolios that maximize expected return for a given level of risk—or equivalently, their portfolios minimize risk for a given level of expected return. Each investor will end up choosing the efficient portfolio that is consistent with his or her utility or risk preferences.

Although this condition may not seem at first glance to be very onerous—people no doubt want the most "bang for their buck"—it actually requires investors to perform the equivalent of a quadratic optimization on a vast number of inputs. We will assume that, despite the difficulties involved, investors do in fact construct relatively efficient portfolios so that the assumption holds, at least approximately.

For large pools of money, the next assumption—that *investments are infinitely divisible*—is close to irrelevant. In constructing an efficient portfolio, the optimal holdings of assets will rarely be round lots. Divisibility would allow an investor to hold fractional amounts of any and all securities. Many investment funds (pensions, mutual

---

[14]The following assumptions generally assume that the "market" is identifiable, when in fact, it is not. Research indicates that the effect of alternative market portfolio assumptions on the beta estimates derived from the CAPM is significant. Those interested in a more complete discussion of the assumptions, or of the CAPM in general, are urged to consult Reilly and Brown (1997, Chapter 9). See also Reilly and Akhtar (1995).

funds, and so forth) are large enough that actual holdings of securities can come very close to the desired efficient portfolio proportions. As was the case with the construction of efficient portfolios, we assume that this requirement holds approximately, with no loss of effectiveness by the CAPM.

The third assumption is that there are *no taxes or transaction costs*. We assume that any taxes and transaction costs have a negligible impact on the CAPM results. This assumption may not be as farfetched as it might seem. Again, consider the large investors that predominate in today's capital markets. For many of them, transaction costs can be minimized through the use of specialized transaction mechanisms and derivatives.

In addition, many of the largest U.S. investors are tax exempt and many non-U.S. investors do not pay capital gains taxes. Thus, a large segment of the investing universe need not pay heed to tax considerations anyway. If transaction costs and taxes were to affect the marginal investor, the results of the model would change somewhat, but the framework and the basic conclusions would remain the same. We assume that these considerations are of second-order importance.

The fourth assumption is that *capital markets are in equilibrium*. Of course, markets may not be in equilibrium at any given time, and securities' prices may not fully reflect all available information. Nevertheless, the CAPM is an equilibrium model, and in setting values and returns that we require from investments, the only appropriate assumption is that markets and securities do move to equilibrium within our time horizon.

In the CAPM, the risk-free rate of interest plays a crucial role. It, in effect, provides the baseline return to which all risk premiums are added. It is also the basis for the fifth assumption, which states that *investors are able to borrow and lend at the (single) risk-free rate*. This condition clearly will not hold when the risk-free rate is a short-term government bill. Investors can lend at that rate, of course, but usually only the government is able to borrow at the risk-free rate. Thus, a small wedge is driven between the borrowing and lending rates.

The sixth assumption is that *all investors have homogeneous expectations*. The standard model requires that their perceptions of risk (although not necessarily their risk tolerances) and their expectations for returns be the same. Thus, everyone has the same pricing model and distributional assumptions, producing a consistent set of outputs—that is, prices or valuations.

If investors price assets in a manner consistent with the CAPM but have differing views on what constitutes their investment market, they will arrive at different conclusions about the riskiness of the assets. Therefore, they can have quite different opinions as to the proper pricing of those assets and their relative attractiveness. In effect, pricing assets in this manner dictates different "equilibrium pricings," whereas no more than one equilibrium can actually hold true. The CAPM does not apply if investors have different expectations. We can still model with a CAPM-like paradigm, but because the market is not in equilibrium, we actually have a factor model.

A seventh required assumption is that *investors fully anticipate the rate of inflation,* so inflation has no real effect on pricing or the equilibrium. If expectations of inflation are perfect, there will be no unintended transfers between users and lenders of capital, no inflation surprises in interest rates and real returns. All returns and real growth rates will simply be augmented by the inflation rate so that the nominal results, less inflation, will be identical to the expected real results. To put the issue more simply, in equilibrium, there is no unexpected inflation.

Although inflation's effects on the CAPM are not directly of interest here, we still consider inflation to be of primary importance. Because we will be presenting a global pricing framework, we will have to deal with currencies in some manner. Inflation differentials bear directly on equilibrium exchange rates.

The final (implicit) assumption of the CAPM is that we are dealing with a *single investment period*. In other words, all investors have the same time horizon and are not considering a multiperiod investment problem. Thus, everyone's risk and return expectations are consistent; no one has different expectations because of a shorter or longer horizon.

CAPM equations. Traditionally, the risk of an asset was taken to be the uncertainty of its expected return. The CAPM, however, breaks risk into two parts: systematic risk and nonmarket, or asset-specific, risk. In equilibrium, only the market risk will be compensated. Any other risk can be eliminated by·holding a diversified portfolio—the market itself. Because nonsystematic risk is avoidable, investors in aggregate neither expect to be nor actually are compensated for taking such risks.

The premium that an asset is expected to earn is a function of its correlation with the market portfolio and the size of its returns relative to the market returns. This relationship is quantified by the asset's beta:

$$\beta_{im} = \frac{\sigma_i}{\sigma_m} \rho_{im}, \tag{13}$$

where σ refers to the uncertainty of the future consumption provided by the asset (i is the asset, m is the aggregate capital market) and ρ_{im} refers to the correlation between the estimate of the asset's consumption flows and the market's consumption flows. The uncertainty about how much future consumption the asset will make available can be proxied by using the asset's cash flow uncertainty. In practice, this exercise is often done with some form of time-series analysis.

Because the risk-free asset (cash) is riskless by definition, it should not earn any compensation for market risk. Thus, its correlations with risky assets and its beta must be zero. The market itself and the risky assets in the market will earn premiums over the risk-free rate as compensation for assuming market risk. For any asset, the expected excess return over the risk-free rate (its risk premium) is proportional to the market's expected excess return. The proportion is given by beta, the amount of nondiversifiable, or market, risk in the asset; formally,

$$r_i - r_f = \beta_{im}(r_m - r_f). \tag{14}$$

In equilibrium, the CAPM provides a framework for developing expected risk premiums and, when combined with an expected risk-free return, expected returns. Substituting Equation 13 for beta and rearranging terms yields

$$r_i - r_f = \sigma_i \rho_{im} \frac{(r_m - r_f)}{\sigma_m}. \tag{15}$$

This equation tells us that the risk premium on an asset is the product of its volatility (risk), its correlation with the market portfolio, and the return per unit of risk to the market portfolio. This last term, the compensation per unit of total risk, is better known as the Sharpe ratio.

The Capital Market Line. Tobin (1958) and Sharpe (1963) demonstrated that the optimal strategy is not merely to identify the portfolio on the efficient frontier that satisfies each investor's risk-tolerance objectives. Rather, they demonstrated that the optimal strategy is to hold the broadly diversified portfolio that affords the highest Sharpe ratio and then combine it with cash to reduce risk to the desirable level or leverage it to increase risk to the desirable level. Combining the highest Sharpe ratio portfolio with cash or leverage provides return and risk combinations that are equal or superior to conventional portfolios on the efficient frontier. Sharpe demonstrated that under the assumptions that underlie the CAPM, all investors will hold the same portfolio, the market portfolio.

The formula for the risk premium, Equation 15, might encourage investors to look for assets with both high volatility and high correlation with the market in order to earn the greatest compensation, rather than holding the market portfolio combined with lending or borrowing. These two objectives, however, are inconsistent.

An efficient portfolio having high correlation with the entire market (say, $\rho = 0.95$) and high risk (assume the portfolio's risk is 20 percent and the market's is 10 percent) would have a beta equal to 1.90; that is, the portfolio's expected excess return would be 1.9 times as large as the expected excess return on the market. If the market's expected risk premium were 2.0 percent, then the portfolio would have an expected premium of 3.8 percent. The premium earned over the risk-free rate would increase to 1.9 times the market's premium, but total risk would also increase—to twice the market's risk. Thus, holding portfolios other than the full market portfolio results in having unnecessarily high levels of risk.

Investors could simply borrow in order to invest in (i.e., leverage) the market portfolio to 1.9 times their capital. (Recall the fifth assumption, that investors can borrow or lend freely at the riskless rate of interest.) The resulting premium would be 1.9 times the unlevered market excess return, or the same 3.8 percent as the portfolio is expected to earn. The risk of this levered market position would only be 1.9 times the unlevered market standard deviation, whereas the portfolio's risk was twice the market's. So, the leveraged market portfolio would have risk of 19 percent compared with the portfolio's 20 percent risk, even though they both have the same expected return.

Figure 19 presents this situation graphically. The aggregate market portfolio and the high-beta portfolio are labeled M and A, respectively. The levered market portfolio is shown as L. It has the same return as Portfolio A (+3.8 percent) but at a lower risk level. Alternatively, the investor could hold a leveraged position with the same risk level as Portfolio A but have a higher expected return. The point attained would be on the straight line directly above A.

The optimal strategy is to identify a portfolio with the same risk as the market portfolio and a correlation of 1 with the market portfolio and then combine that portfolio with cash or leverage it to achieve the desired risk level. Only one portfolio satisfies those constraints: the market portfolio. All investors will, therefore, hold the market portfolio combined with lending or borrowing.

By holding some fraction of wealth in the risk-free asset, with return R_f, and the remainder in the full market, the investor can achieve any of the points along the line between R_f and M. Likewise, by borrowing at R_f and increasing exposure to the market portfolio, the investor can increase risk and return, moving along the line beyond the market portfolio. This line is known as the Capital Market Line. It describes (in a forward-looking equilibrium) the most efficient risk–return trade-offs available. In fact, the slope of the Capital Market Line is the market portfolio's Sharpe ratio—the incremental return earned for each additional unit of market risk assumed. The Capital Market Line describes the highest attainable Sharpe ratio; all other portfolios are less efficient—that is, have less return per unit of risk assumed.

Figure 19. Capital Market Line

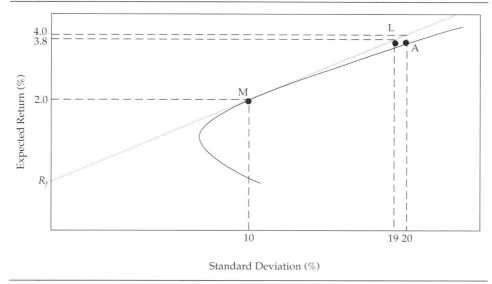

This example pertains to a high-beta portfolio, A, rather than a single asset. In equilibrium, single securities will almost certainly lie inside the curved (efficient) frontier. Thus, the advantages of holding the market portfolio in combination with the riskless asset are even greater compared with single assets.

If the assumptions of the CAPM hold, all investors will have the same view of the opportunities and risks in the globally integrated capital market. Therefore, the Capital Market Line will be the same for all investors. Recall from the assumptions that, although they have consistent expectations, all investors are not required to have the same risk tolerance. Figure 20 shows two different investors' utility curves and desired portfolios; their portfolios will always be composed of the market portfolio and the riskless asset. Investor 1 (utility curve U_1) is more risk averse than Investor 2 (utility curve U_2) and, therefore, holds a substantial amount of cash (riskless asset). Investor 1's portfolio provides expected risk and return given by Point P_1. Investor 2, in contrast, has very low risk aversion and actually borrows, paying R_f, in order to hold more than 100 percent of his or her investment capital in the market portfolio.

Figure 20. Investor Preferences

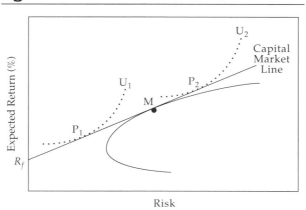

Multicurrency CAPM. The CAPM framework can also be applied to allocating the global capital market return. First, however, three important issues need to be addressed: How is the risk-free rate defined, how should currencies be handled, and what constitutes the market portfolio of risky assets?

Short-term instruments and the "risk-free" return. Most short-term financial instruments can be considered claims on capital, so they should participate in the aggregate capital market return. For the most part, though, short-term assets are considered virtually riskless. A true riskless asset provides a certain return rather than a distribution of returns.

Generally, short-term instruments such as U.S. Treasury bills, Eurodeposits, and commercial paper provide only the real risk-free return and an inflation premium. A risk premium, when it exists, is likely to be small. For financial assets of short duration, inflation uncertainty is not an important factor; credit risk (uncertainty about whether principal and income can be fully paid) produces small risk premiums.

Over very short periods of time, a riskless asset can exist. Even over longer horizons, short-term assets are close to riskless in the following sense: Because the interest rate is able to adjust without causing capital gains or losses, the inflation premium can change, leaving the real return in equilibrium. (Technically, the CAPM is a single-period model and the risk-free return is known perfectly in advance.) Realized real risk-free returns are essentially equal to those expected at the start of the period. Given realized real returns equal to expected returns, the value of future consumption obtained by holding cash should be equal to its expected value. Longer-dated bonds, zero-coupon bonds in particular, are riskless in nominal terms (assuming no credit risk) but have considerable risk in real terms because the actual inflation between now and their maturity is unknown.[15]

What is the appropriate instrument to use as the riskless asset? Many researchers use short-term T-bills, but this approach has several drawbacks. In many countries other than the United States, short-term treasury securities do not exist or their characteristics are quite different from those of U.S. instruments.[16] To obviate this problem, we used three-month Eurodeposits as the riskless asset. Eurodeposits have the advantage of uniformity across countries and nearly universal availability, at least in developed markets. From a global perspective, having a consistent riskless asset is a distinct advantage. In a global multicurrency framework, Eurodeposit rates are attractive for another reason: They are used in pricing forward currency transactions.

Because Euros are contracts with banks or other financial institutions, the yields quoted (and thus the returns provided), in fact, include some amount of risk premium. If government bills are considered truly riskless (which is a pretty questionable assumption for some countries), then a Euro must have some credit risk: The bank or other party to the contract might not pay at maturity. Outside the United States, these credit spreads are small, which again points to the appropriateness of using the Euro rate to represent the riskless asset.

---

[15]Recently introduced inflation-indexed U.S. Treasury bonds provide alternative observations of risk-free rates of interest. They provide a riskless real return for investment horizons equal to the maturity of the instrument.

[16]U.S. T-bills may, in fact, trade *below* the risk-free rate. Because of special considerations such as collateral and reserve requirements, T-bills may have nonmarket demand that reduces their interest rate below the risk-free rate. This result is evidenced by a Treasury–Eurodeposit (TED) spread that is much higher in the United States than elsewhere.

One additional advantage that the Eurodeposit rate has over the government bill rate is its availability to institutional investors. Remember that one of the assumptions of the CAPM is that investors are able to borrow and lend at the riskless rate of interest. This assumption was used in the model to develop the Capital Market Line. If the T-bill represents the riskless asset, then we must allow for different borrowing and lending rates. Of course, investors can always lend to the government at that rate, but only the government can borrow at such a low rate of interest. Most large institutional investors can both borrow and lend at Eurodeposit rates.

So, for both theoretical and practical purposes, we used Euros as the riskless asset and omitted from the risky portfolio those assets slated to repay principal within a one-year time frame. Most market participants consider short-dated assets to be the functional equivalent of cash substitutes. Aside from these theoretical considerations, in many countries, market capitalization data are difficult or impossible to obtain for instruments of less than one year in maturity. So, in constructing the market portfolio, we will eliminate any (fixed-income) security with less than a year remaining to its life.

Currencies and inflation. In a global setting, currency movements (i.e., exchange rate returns) can affect the returns earned on nondomestic assets. Therefore, we need to know the impact on the CAPM of assets denominated in different currencies.

The primary underlying framework for currency in equilibrium is based on purchasing power parity (PPP). Because the model is an equilibrium model (i.e., CAPM for the markets and assets), we need to have an exchange rate equilibrium as well. A PPP equilibrium can be defined simply as a condition in which a good, service, or real or financial asset purchased with a certain amount of currency in one country will cost the same in any other country, after translation into the base currency. Flexible exchange rates, as well as prices of goods, services, and assets, adjust to maintain the relationship. In a fixed or pegged exchange rate regime, only the prices of goods, services, and assets adjust.[17]

Although PPP is not useful in predicting the direction of exchange rates over the short term, over long periods of time, exchange rates do move toward PPP equilibrium levels. Apart from legal, cultural, and economic barriers, trade and capital flows create pressure to equilibrate the prices of goods, services, and assets among countries. True (or absolute) PPP requires that the prices of identical goods, services, and assets be the same in all countries. A weaker form of PPP, relative PPP, states only that exchange rates move to offset inflation differences. Of course, if absolute PPP holds, then relative PPP does also.

Figure 21 compares the actual U.K. pound sterling/U.S. dollar exchange rate with two alternative PPP measures. In this case, the purchasing power exchange rate is based on wholesale price indexes in the countries, with movements in the real exchange rate index defined by the inflation differential. The first measure, the centered PPP exchange rate, is derived from making the average of the PPP exchange rate equal to the average actual exchange rate, with movements in the PPP rate dependent on the inflation differential. The second measure, the regression PPP exchange rate, is constructed by setting the average real exchange rate index to the average nominal

---

[17]The equivalence of prices of identical goods across countries and currencies is also known as the "Law of One Price." In practice, studies of PPP often focus on traded goods only, because the pressures toward price equalization of nontraded goods and services are indirect and less intense than those for traded goods. In the presence of free movement of labor or capital, however, equilibrium would entail similar prices for any good, service, or asset regardless of location.

Figure 21. Pound Sterling/U.S. Dollar Exchange Rates, 1900–96

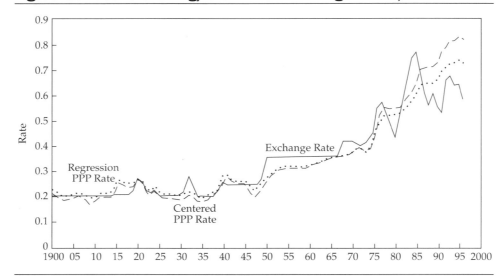

exchange rate over the full period.[18] Thus, the average for the regression PPP exchange rate is the same as the average actual exchange rate, with the direction of the PPP rate dependent on the slope coefficient of the regression and on the inflation differential between the United States and the United Kingdom. The slope coefficient accounts for potential measurement biases in each country's inflation measure.

The figure makes clear that exchange rates often deviate from PPP levels, and the deviations can be quite large and prolonged. These deviations have many potential causes, many of them falling under the rubric of capital flows. Over time, however, the general trend is the same in both the exchange rate and the inflation differential, so there is no long-run trend toward higher real prices in one country relative to the other.

Notice that we did not say that the exchange rate adjusts to the inflation differential, because the exchange rate is not necessarily the dependent variable. Although floating exchange rates allow the nominal exchange rate to change in order to equalize prices across countries, in a world of fixed exchange rates, the adjustment must occur through other means. If the exchange rate does not move to equalize prices, prices must adjust instead. Thus, the country with the "cheaper" goods, services, or assets (translated into the other's currency) must experience higher inflation than its counterpart. For example, in a world of fixed exchange rates, if domestic prices rise (say, because of a monetary shock), foreign goods will be cheaper than domestic goods. Demand for goods, services, and assets will increase in the foreign economy, with a concomitant flow of money. Because the exchange rate is fixed, the increase in demand will send foreign prices upward. This adjustment process will proceed until absolute PPP is restored.[19]

Because the long-run pressures are toward PPP, we define equilibrium as equivalence of prices across countries and currencies and require that the nominal exchange rate move by the inflation differential. This equilibrium can be modified to account for considerations such as trade balances, capital flows, and other sustained pressures.

---

[18]Logarithmic (continuously compounded) returns were used in the regression in order to account for the trend resulting from the inflation differential.

[19]We have greatly simplified a number of points here, particularly the issue of traded versus nontraded goods and the monetary adjustment mechanism under a fixed exchange regime.

Figure 22 presents another way to look at this relationship. Each point on the figure represents a separate country. The *y* coordinate represents the annual change in the country's currency relative to the U.S. dollar, and the *x* coordinate gives its annualized consumer price inflation relative to U.S. inflation. During this period of more than 20 years from June 1973 to March 1997, most of the points plot fairly close to the diagonal line. If a point fell directly on the line, the change in exchange rate equaled the inflation differential. We can see that most currencies moved to offset inflation differences, meaning that relative PPP tends to hold over long periods of time. Because most points lie slightly below the line, the U.S. dollar has depreciated somewhat more than is implied by inflation differentials.

Figure 22. Rates of Change in Consumer Price Differentials and Exchange Rates

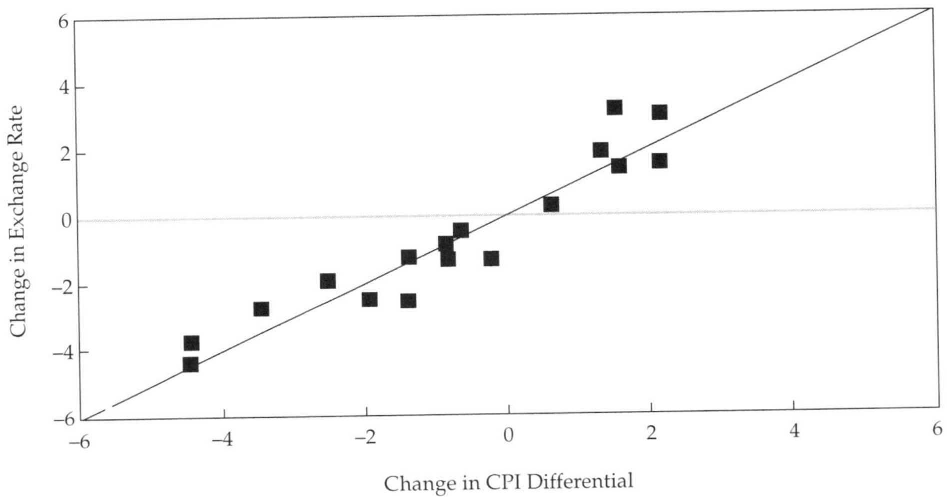

Note: Based on log returns from June 30, 1973, to September 30, 1996.

Figure 23 demonstrates that the result is the same if the exercise is done with producer rather than consumer price indexes. Here again, the U.S. dollar has been slightly weaker than would be true if PPP held throughout the period. Nonetheless, the general pattern of exchange rates offsetting inflation differentials is still apparent.

The fact that exchange rates tend to move in the direction implied by PPP is important in an equilibrium investment framework. In equilibrium, exchange rates should offset any inflation differentials, so identical assets in different countries with different inflation rates should have identical real returns.[20]

The global risk-free rate. In describing the CAPM, we made no explicit assumptions about the investor's base currency or the currencies in which assets might be denominated. The implicit assumption was that the model is applied to assets denominated in the investor's base currency, because the risk-free rate (used to derive the risk premiums) was the investor's domestic cash rate. In moving from the basic CAPM equation to a global CAPM framework, what is the risk-free rate? What is the appropriate risk-free rate to use in setting the market's risk premium in a global model if assets are denominated in more than one currency?

---

[20]This relationship would also include the equivalence of the real risk-free return among countries. There should be no advantage to holding riskless cash in another currency.

Figure 23. Rates of Change in Producer Price Differentials and Exchange Rates

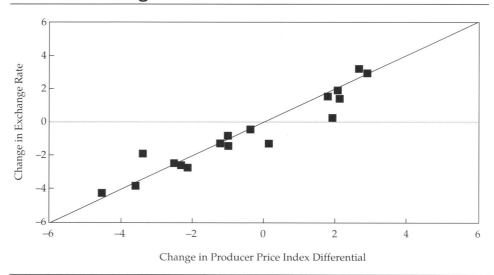

Note: Based on log returns from June 30, 1973, to September 30, 1996.

Under equilibrium conditions, the CAPM does not need to change, because any asset's risk premium is equal to its return less its local cash rate. These risk premiums are then independent of currency and are the same irrespective of an investor's base currency. This relationship is valid under both hedged and unhedged conditions. [21]

In a world with different currencies, an investor with exposure to a foreign asset generally has an equally large exposure to the currency in which the asset is denominated. Thus, in addition to the asset's risk, there is also the risk of fluctuations in the exchange rate. U.S.-based investors holding British gilts face the risk posed by changes in the level and shape of the yield curve in Britain. They are also exposed to movements in the pound/dollar exchange rate. An investor holding a foreign asset cannot earn the local-currency return (unless, of course, the exchange rate remains fixed against the domestic currency). The return to the investor is equal to the foreign local return less the percentage change in the exchange rate:

$$\text{Return} = R_{\pounds} - \%\Delta\varepsilon_{\pounds/\$}, \tag{16}$$

where $R_{\pounds}$ is the local return and $\%\Delta\varepsilon_{\pounds/\$}$ is the change in the exchange rate, expressed as foreign currency per U.S. dollar. [22]

- *The unhedged case.* Define the cash return in the United States, $c_{\$}$, as the sum of a real risk-free return, rf_r, plus an inflation rate, P:

$$c_{\$} = rf_r + \%\Delta P_{\$}. \tag{17}$$

In a globally integrated world, the real risk-free rate will be constant among all countries. In addition, we know from PPP equilibrium that the change in the exchange rate is equal to the difference in inflation rates; that is,

$$\%\Delta\varepsilon_{\pounds/\$} = \%\Delta P_{\pounds} - \%\Delta P_{\$}, \tag{18}$$

---

[21]To arrive at this conclusion requires some mathematical manipulation. Although we believe that an understanding of why the transformation works is very useful, the math-disinclined reader can skip the derivation. See Karnosky and Singer (1994, Section I).

[22]To simplify the exposition, we will assume that the dollar is the investor's base currency and the foreign currency is the pound sterling. The approach is easily generalized to any base and foreign currency.

where the exchange rate is defined as pounds sterling per dollar. If we rearrange Equation 18 and substitute dollar cash (Equation 17) for U.S. inflation in the equation, we get

$$c_\$ = r_{fr} + \%\Delta P_\pounds - \%\Delta\varepsilon_{\pounds/\$}. \tag{19}$$

Using Equation 16, except defined in terms of U.K. inflation and cash, this relationship can be simplified to

$$c_\$ = c_\pounds - \%\Delta\varepsilon_{\pounds/\$}. \tag{20}$$

The cash rate in the United Kingdom is simply equal to the cash rate in the United States plus the change in the exchange rate. This relationship is known as "uncovered interest parity." In equilibrium, all riskless assets will deliver to the investor a return of the real risk-free rate plus a domestic inflation premium.

Turning to the return on a U.K. risky asset, translated into dollars, we define the total return as

$$R_{UK}^{\$} = R_{UK}^{\pounds} - \%\Delta\varepsilon_{\pounds/\$}, \tag{21}$$

where the superscript denotes the currency in which the return is denominated and the subscript (in this case, *UK*) denotes the asset. The return is simply the asset's local-currency return adjusted for exchange rate changes.

If we rearrange the uncovered interest parity condition (Equation 20) and substitute for the exchange rate in Equation 21, we get

$$R_{UK}^{\$} = R_{UK}^{\pounds} + (c_\$ - c_\pounds), \text{ or}$$
$$R_{UK}^{\$} - c_\$ = R_{UK}^{\pounds} - c_\pounds. \tag{22}$$

This equation tells us that the premium over cash that the U.S. investor should expect to earn is exactly the same as the risk premium that the British investor expects. The premium on the asset is independent of both the investor's base currency and the asset's currency of denomination.

Therefore, in equilibrium, the risk premium on an unhedged asset, no matter what its base currency or the currency into which it is translated, is equal to the local return less the local cash return.

- *The hedged case.* Currency risk for most developed markets can be eliminated with hedges, such as forwards, futures, and swaps. Hedge construction is straightforward: The investor gives up the return on foreign cash and, in exchange, receives the return on domestic cash. Thus, the effect of a hedge is $c_\$ - c_\pounds$.

A hedge affects the returns earned on the foreign assets. If the yield on foreign cash is greater than the domestic yield, the investor must pay the difference. If the foreign cash yield is less than the domestic, the investor benefits from the differential. Therefore, the investor's return on a hedged foreign asset is

$$R_{UK}^{\$} = R_{UK}^{\pounds} + (c_\$ - c_\pounds). \tag{23}$$

This equation is exactly the same as that obtained in the unhedged case. So, the equilibrium risk premium that an asset provides is invariant to the decision about whether to hedge.[23]

---

[23]The "effect of the hedge" can also be written as the difference between the forward exchange rate and the spot exchange rate. When expressed in this fashion, the equation is known as the "covered interest parity" condition. Under PPP, both covered and uncovered interest parity must hold.

Indeed, one major implication of this approach is that all investors can analyze their assets in risk premium terms. When hedging is available, the market decision can be separated from the currency decision, granting the investor the ability to manage market and currency exposures separately. There is no fundamental reason why the asset or market allocation should be married to the currency exposure decision (that is not to say that expected market returns may not be affected by exchange rate movements or valuation considerations).

Given the ability to hedge away any short-run currency risks, there still must be some framework for evaluating which currency exposures to take. All currency exposure cannot be eliminated; if all the foreign currency exposure is hedged away, the investor simply has 100 percent exposure to the domestic currency. Although this position may be one of low risk, it is not a position of no exposure.

The model. In the multicurrency framework, the market portfolio includes assets denominated in many different currencies. We have shown that in equilibrium, every asset's risk premium is independent of both the currency in which it is denominated and the investor's base currency. Thus, in defining the aggregate risk premium on the market portfolio, we need not be concerned with the base currency, only the relative weights of the components. The market's aggregate risk premium is simply the weighted average of the constituent assets' premiums.

The risk-free return for each investor remains the sum of the global real risk-free return and the investor's base inflation premium. The risk premium on any asset is the same, however, regardless of the investor's base currency. Therefore, in a multi-currency setting, the CAPM equation becomes

$$RP_i = \beta_{im}(RP_m) \tag{24}$$

when the local risk-free rate has been subtracted from the local return to produce the risk premium, RP_i.

Using Equation 13—the definition of beta—we can write the CAPM equation as

$$RP_i = \frac{\sigma_i}{\sigma_m} \rho_{im}(RP_m)$$
$$= \sigma_i \rho_{im} \frac{RP_m}{\sigma_m}. \tag{25}$$

This last equation is the multicurrency CAPM used in our empirical analysis.[24] It describes the risk premium that an asset provides as a function of the asset's standard deviation, its correlation with the global market portfolio, and the global market's Sharpe ratio—the aggregate compensation per unit of risk. Because the market portfolio is the capitalization-weighted average of the components, the market's aggregate risk premium will be the weighted average of the component assets' risk premiums.

Relaxing the assumptions of the CAPM. Up to this point, we have assumed that the CAPM holds, that the model's assumptions are not violated. But, not all investors perceive the same market portfolio. In addition, exchange rates often drift quite far from equilibrium, or PPP, rates.

The CAPM assumes that all investors hold efficient portfolios; therefore, only the market portfolio can be efficient. When different investors use different market portfolios in their anayses, this assumption is no longer valid. Moreover, different market

---

[24]Clearly, this multicurrency CAPM is no different from a domestic CAPM because in equilibrium, the denomination of the nominal cash rate is irrelevant.

portfolio perceptions result in divergent expectations regarding systematic risk.

Consider a simple case in which "global" investors take the market portfolio to be the fully integrated global portfolio and "home" investors' market portfolios are based on segmentation of capital markets and are overly skewed to the domestic bond market.

Each type of investor views the riskiness of the home investor's bond market differently, although we assume that risk has the same price for both investors. In the context of a well-diversified portfolio, the riskiness of the bond market is smaller than when viewed narrowly. Although the volatility risk of the bond market is the same to both investors, to the global investor, the systematic portion of the market risk is relatively small because of the diversity of assets held. Therefore, the global investor is likely to attach a relatively low risk premium to that bond market. To the home-biased investor, the bond market is risky because his or her "market" portfolio lacks diversification. This investor views a large portion of the bond market's risk as systematic, so the risk premium will be commensurately large.

Clearly, the risk premium cannot be simultaneously small and large. The bond market is likely to be priced so that the risk premium and return are relatively attractive to the global investor and unattractive to the home investor. In effect, the home investor is pricing a risk factor—home-biased market portfolio risk—that is irrelevant to the global investor. Thus, the global investor's risk premium exceeds that required to compensate for the risk of the market.

For our purposes, we used a CAPM-like factor model and assumed that various degrees of integration are viable. The market portfolio was varied to reflect full integration, regional integration, home-biased integration, and full market segmentation. The result is a range of risk premiums that tend to be lowest for the fully integrated case and highest for the fully segmented case. The appropriate market-equilibrating risk premium requires a forward-looking assessment of capital market integration.

The second deviation from CAPM assumptions that we address is the failure of PPP. When PPP does not hold, capital markets fail to be in equilibrium and a single risk-free rate of interest does not prevail. Investors in different countries will face different cash rates, and returns on foreign cash can be above or below those on domestic cash, even after taking exchange rate movements into account. The real exchange rate becomes important and can enter into the pricing of, and returns to, holding nondomestic assets. From a pricing model perspective, the result is a factor model that also includes a real exchange rate factor; that is,

$$RP_i = b_{im} + \sum_j b_{ij} I_j, \tag{26}$$

where b_{im} corresponds to a market factor sensitivity, I_j is a set of real exchange-rate-related factors, and b_{ij} represents the asset's sensitivity to the exchange rate factors.

We did not use this version of the pricing model because it requires long-term expectations of exchange rate disequilibriums. We assumed that exchange rate equilibrium holds in the long run and, therefore, did not price the exchange rate factors.

2. Empirical Examination of Capital Market Returns

The return to any asset is a combination of a real risk-free rate, an inflation premium, and a risk premium. The real risk-free rate is compensation for parting with capital, regardless of where the funds are invested. As such, the real risk-free rate is the same for every asset. The inflation premium is compensation for the decline in buying power that might result from price inflation. The inflation premium is independent of the investment vehicle but dependent on the investor's consumption basket. Finally, the risk premium provides compensation for the uncertainty surrounding the future consumption that an asset is expected to provide. Risk premiums differ across assets, in that they provide investors with different expected future consumption patterns and different risks.

In this chapter, we apply the theoretical framework to developing long-term forecasts for the real risk-free rate, the inflation premium, and the aggregate and individual market risk premiums. To develop the market and asset-class risk premiums, we determined the global price of risk (the global capital market Sharpe ratio) and applied it to various integrated and segmented measures of risk. For the purpose of this analysis, we focused on the Canadian, German, Japanese, U.K., and U.S. equity and debt markets.

The Real Risk-Free Rate

The simple model for estimating the real risk-free rate is based on consumption time preferences and economic productivity. In the short term, many factors can influence each of these determinants. In the long term, however, demographic developments, broad cultural trends, and large shifts in economic structure are of paramount importance. Short-term influences are also important, of course, but they are not the focus of this monograph.

Long-term trends in consumption time preferences can be gauged to some extent by evaluating demographic trends. Typically, the working-age portion of the population spans from about 15 years to 65 years of age. We are interested in comparing that portion of the working-age population that is characterized by saving behavior, 30–65 year olds, with that portion that focuses on consumption, those older than 65.[25] The under-30 age category is omitted because the consumption patterns of people in that age group vary considerably between industrial and developing economies. In industrial economies, individuals entering the workforce often incur debt as they purchase houses and automobiles. Young people in developing economies, however, are less able to pursue this dis-saving behavior. In addition, the youngest portion of the population is typically dependent, so their consumption behavior is difficult to disentangle from that of their parents; they are difficult to classify as either saving or consuming.

---

[25]We use the term consumption somewhat loosely to denote behavior associated with drawing down savings, or dis-saving. (Of course, all people must consume in order to survive; what is at issue is the degree of consumption relative to income.)

Figure 24 shows that the narrowly defined working-age portion of the population is declining in both developed and developing countries. The large disparity in ratios, however, indicates a major difference between these two groups in the relative desires to save and consume, which creates a strong incentive to integrate the economies of these broad groups. Any time a voluntary exchange can occur—in this case, shifting savings to regions where savings are more highly valued—welfare should increase. This process appears to have driven some of the recent frenzy toward economic integration: the European Monetary Union, the North American Free Trade Agreement, the Association of South East Asian Nations, expansion of capital flows to and from emerging markets, and so forth. The sustainability of this trend depends on the disparity between time preferences of consumption.

If the proportion of a country's working-age population is relatively high, the country has a propensity toward saving for future consumption. A low percentage indicates a greater propensity toward current consumption. Demographic trends in developed countries indicate that a growing proportion of the population is in the dissaving age bracket, which as Figure 25 shows, puts upward pressure on the real risk-free rate because of an increase in the marginal rate of substitution between current and future consumption.

Although the fact that the working-age population is generally declining could be taken as a signal of upward pressure on the real risk-free rate, the process of integration should place downward rather than upward pressure on the real rate in the industrial countries. As the greater savings propensity from the developing countries is combined with the lower ratio of working-age to retired population in developed countries, expectations of a stagnant-to-declining real risk-free rate may be more appropriate.

Economic integration is likely to increase global productive capacity by rectifying suboptimal resource allocations. Congruent with the evolution in time preferences of consumption, the economywide production-possibility frontier is likely to expand. The introduction of untapped resources of less-skilled labor from the developing markets enables all resources to be used more efficiently. The result is a more productive global economy and a more steeply sloped production-possibility frontier.

Figure 24. Ratio of Saving Age to Consuming Age: Developed and Developing Countries, 1950–2024

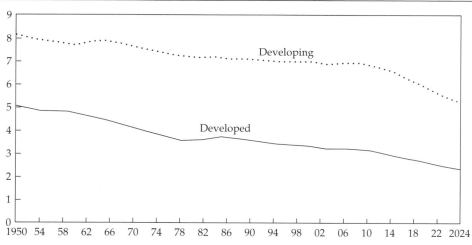

©The Research Foundation of the ICFA

**Figure 25. Effects of Upward Pressure on Real
Risk-Free Rate: Developed Countries**

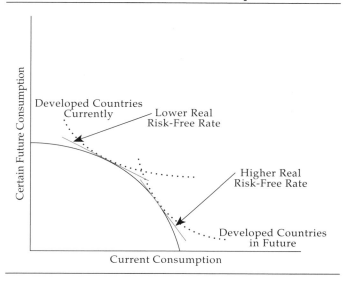

Figure 26 reflects the combined influence of these developments. Given the size of developed economies relative to developing economies, the effect of economic integration is likely to begin at a slow rate with relatively small time preference, productivity, and real risk-free rate implications. The process of evolution would involve a shift from the current status of present and future consumption of the world, represented by Point A, toward the future status, represented by Point B.[26] This exaggerated shift reflects both the increased productivity and the increased propensity to save derived from the integration of developing economies. The small relative economic size of developing countries suggests that the future marginal propensity to save is likely to reside close to Point A.

This analysis is inconclusive regarding the future level of the real risk-free rate; clearly, however, an anticipated increase in that rate based on analysis of developed economies is not necessarily warranted. How then might we gauge the level of the real risk-free rate?

Figure 27 shows the year-by-year level of the U.S. real risk-free rate based on 30-day U.S. Treasury bills deflated by the U.S. Consumer Price Index (CPI). The rate fluctuates around an average of about 0.7 percent, tracing a pattern that provides historical documentation of periods of war, oil shocks, and so forth. Since World War II, the average real rate has been about 0.8 percent.[27]

T-bills are affected by a variety of factors that may, in fact, indicate that the historically derived real risk-free rate is too low. Figure 28 shows the same spread over a shorter period for the 30-day T-bill and three-month Eurodollar rates, also deflated by the CPI. The average T-bill-based real risk-free rate is 1.4 percent, and the average three-month Eurodollar rate is 2.9 percent over this period, reflecting both credit and maturity spreads over the T-bill rate. The credit spread was relatively wide because of the many financial institution crises during the late 1970s and early 1980s.

---

[26]Strictly speaking, Point A is not representative of the world, simply that portion participating in the financial or capital markets.

[27]The fact that the CPI may be a biased indicator of true or underlying inflation has only minor importance in this analysis. In using historical data, adjusting for the bias would reduce the inflation rate and increase the real return by the same amount. The risk-free rate (return to cash) would remain the same; only its measured composition would change.

Figure 26. Effects of Saving Ratio and Productive Capacity on Real Risk-Free Rate

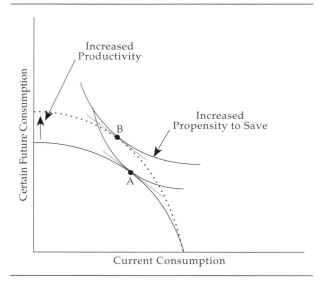

Figure 27. U.S. Annual Real Risk-Free Rate, Based on 30-Day T-Bill Rate Less Consumer Price Inflation, 1925–96

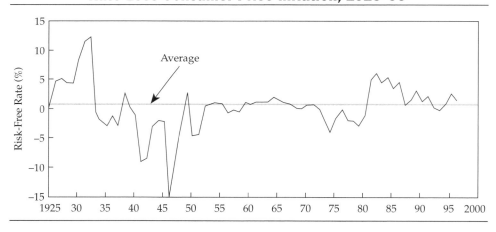

Figure 28. U.S. Annual Real Risk-Free and Eurodeposit Rates, Based on Cash Less Consumer Price Inflation, 1970–96

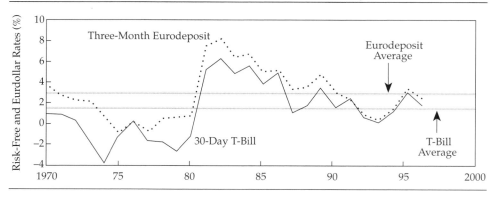

On a global basis, the average Eurodeposit-based real risk-free rate averaged about 2.7 percent between 1971 and 1995, following the pattern evident in Figure 29. Applying similar credit and maturity considerations to the global data suggests a global real risk-free rate somewhat less than 2.7 percent. Productivity and demographic trends suggest a long-term, pretax Eurodeposit-based real risk-free rate of about 2.0 percent. Obviously, variation around this estimate has been and is likely to be substantial, but we assume that 2.0 percent is a good indication of central tendency over the long term.

Figure 29. Global Annual Risk-Free Rate, Based on Three-Month Eurodeposits Less Consumer Price Index, 1971–96

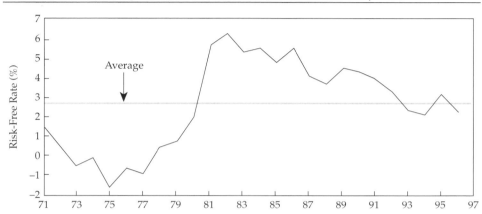

The Inflation Premium

According to the quantity theory of money, an increase in the money supply results in an increase either in prices or in real output, or a decrease in velocity. Applying this relationship to an individual country, we can portray historical data according to this paradigm and make long-term forecasts for growth and inflation that are consistent, given some understanding of monetary policy.

In the United States, M1, although increasing in volatility in recent years, has settled into a long-term growth rate of about 5–8 percent (see Figure 11). Looking forward, central bank actions appear to be more consistent with a stable price objective rather than a growth objective, despite the fact that the stated objectives include both price stability and growth.

Velocity growth was high in the 1970s, declined in the early 1980s, and has been relatively stable at zero since then (see Figure 10). Velocity was probably significantly influenced by an increasing opportunity cost of holding narrow money balances in the 1970s and by decreasing cost in the early 1980s. An absence of trends in interest rates in the future should produce a trendless velocity. In other words, as long as short-term interest rates show no upward trend, velocity growth should vary around zero.

Taking moderate real growth into consideration, together with no trend in velocity, a controlled monetary expansion in the mid-single digits will produce a long-term inflation rate of less than 3 percent. We assumed a U.S. inflation rate of 2.75 percent, which is similar to that experienced in recent years. Although the business cycle has not ended, Federal Reserve policy has shifted more toward price stability than during the 1970s. This policy will be implemented in a consistent manner going forward.

This analysis can be applied on a country-by-country basis to develop secular inflation forecasts in each market. Among the nonquantitative considerations is the fact that central banks globally are evolving toward and institutionalizing independence of the monetary authority and specifying price stability rather than growth objectives. Legislative proposals in Belgium, Canada, Denmark, France, Italy, the Netherlands, New Zealand, and Spain exemplify the move toward greater central bank independence. The breadth of this movement is confirmed by similar tendencies in many developing countries.

Capital markets, as the rational expectations model of inflation expectations would suggest, have become punitive toward markets in countries where the monetary authority acts in a manner other than that implied by an objective of price stability. Increasingly, people vote with their mobile capital rather than with their relatively immobile feet. Estimates of long-term secular inflation are 2.75 percent for Canada, 2.25 percent for Germany, 1.70 percent for Japan, and 3.00 percent for the United Kingdom.

We also computed an aggregate world inflation rate. Although this exercise may seem counterintuitive, given the multitude of currencies and the inflation-equilibrating nature of exchange rates, world inflation can be expressed in terms of a world currency unit (a global basket of all currencies). In equilibrium, world inflation, expressed in world currency unit terms, is equal to the weighted-average local-currency inflation of every country in the world. We estimate a future aggregate world inflation rate of 2.9 percent.

Global Capital Market Price of Risk

Developing risk premiums for each individual equity and bond market requires an estimate of the compensation the market requires for incurring risk. From estimates of the market's risk premium and its risk in a globally integrated framework, we estimated the standard deviation of the global capital market. The global price of risk (the risk premium per unit of risk) is the Sharpe ratio of the global capital market. From the Sharpe ratio, the risk premium on each asset class can be computed based on its systematic risk.

The Global Risk Premium. The expected long-term real return available to a globally integrated capital market is equal to the global net capital market income yield (reflecting a world inflation premium of 2.9 percent) plus the expected long-term real growth rate of the economy. The net income yield is aggregate global capital market income less decrements to this income stream in the form of net new issuance; that is,

$$R_r = \left[\left(\frac{I_K}{W_K} \right) - \left(\frac{N_1}{W_K} \right) \right] + G_r. \tag{27}$$

We approached this investigation in the three stages corresponding to the three components of the aggregate real return available to capital markets. We first estimated future world real growth (G_r) looking forward.[28] Second, we derived an estimate of the first-period world capital market income level (I_K/W_K). Third, we estimated the level of world net new issuance (N_1/W_K). Although this estimate is no more or less important than the other two, its complexity and the associated data limitations compel us to discuss our methods in detail. If we were discussing real assets rather than securitized assets, net new issuance would be zero. All income flows to human capital and land and capital goods owners would be in terms of cash flows. Only in the case of financial assets can cash income be augmented or reduced through the net new

---

[28]The growth rate used here, the economy's real growth, should not be confused with other notions of growth, such as earnings growth, that are often the focus of financial research.

issuance of claims. Because we are forced to consider claims on real assets, we also must take into account any compensation that arises from negative net new issuance.

World Real Growth. Table 2 shows annual real GDP growth from 1947 to 1996 and estimates of the long-term future real growth expected in each region and in the world. This set of estimates is based on economic assumptions that we believe are appropriate, although another analyst might take issue with any or all of them. Heterogeneous expectations, after all, are what make investment opportunities.

Although we used historical data as a starting point in developing forecasts of real growth, we do not adhere to any misconception that gross domestic product is an accurate measure of growth. In fact, GDP, especially in recent decades, has underestimated underlying economic growth. The primary obstacle to measuring real growth is accounting for changes in the quality of the goods and services produced. A luxury car of the 1990s has substantial advantages over a car that "comes in any color as long as it's black."

Services are a growing portion of the economy; both industry and agriculture are declining shares. U.S. employment in the service sector accounts for nearly 75 percent of total employment, and industry and agriculture combined account for a little more than 25 percent. Service-sector output is much more difficult to measure than the tangible items that dominate national income accounting methodologies.

Measured productivity growth has slowed, largely because of the service sector. Manufacturing productivity growth, which can be more accurately measured, has sustained a better rate. Although a unit of output in the service sector is difficult to measure, it is hard believe that recent investments in information technology have failed to boost or at least sustain service-sector productivity growth (see Griliches 1994).

The statistical problem *du jour* is that price indexes are generally perceived to overstate inflation because quality changes are inadequately captured and consumption baskets do not sufficiently adjust for substitution. If price changes are overstated, then real growth is probably understated.

A number of basic observations can be made from Table 2. First, the future real rate of world growth is likely to be somewhat higher than reported growth during the past 50 years, in part reflecting the distinction between GDP as a measure of growth and underlying real economic growth. Second, the pattern of more rapid growth in

Table 2. World Real Growth by Region

Region	GDP Growth 1947–96[a]	Estimated Future Growth
OECD	3.5%	3.0%
North America	3.0	3.0
Western Europe	3.7	3.0
Japan	6.3	3.0
Australia and New Zealand	3.8	3.0
Non-oil-producing developing countries	5.8	6.8
Far East (including China)	7.7	8.0
South Asia	4.2	6.5
Latin America	4.6	5.5
Sub-Saharan Africa	3.1	3.5
Mideast/North Africa	5.6	4.5
Organization of Petroleum Exporting Countries	5.1	4.0
Eastern Europe/Commonwealth of Independent States	2.5	4.5
World	3.9	4.0

[a]Based on data from NAE Associates.

developing economies than in developed economies is not likely to change. This pattern reflects a strong incentive that has been and will continue to be in place for increasing global economic integration. The process of becoming more integrated should produce faster growth in developing countries as financial and human capital become more available to them. Once the developing countries become fully integrated into the global economy (by definition, they would no longer be developing at that stage), economic growth rates should converge. Third, convergence of economic growth in developed countries will occur despite admittedly important differences arising from government policies, which may interfere with or smooth the functioning of goods, services, and asset markets.

First-Period World Capital Market Income. Because current market capitalization may be either above or below the fundamental value of the underlying capital market assets, an estimate of capital market income based only on current dividend and coupon information is likely to be biased.[29] Estimates of equilibrium capital market income in nominal terms amount to 3.0 percent for the global equity market, 5.7 percent for the global bond market, and 4.9 percent for the two combined.

A bond in a high-inflation country will tend to pay a higher coupon than an otherwise similar bond in a low-inflation country. Each coupon reflects an inflation premium appropriate for the currency of denomination of the bond. To show income data on a world basis, all income data must be converted from the local-currency expected rate of inflation to the world rate of inflation. We accomplished this adjustment by subtracting from each country's normalized dividend and coupon rates an estimate of long-term inflation in that country and adding in a long-term world inflation rate.

Net New Issuance. The cash flow stream to a claim on wealth—an equity or bond—can come in the form of a stated payment, such as a dividend or coupon, or in the form of security redemptions, such as stock buybacks or bond calls or maturities. Net new issuance is the mirror image of these redemptions and is, therefore, subtracted from the stated cash flow to obtain the total income stream.

The segmentation of net new issuance into U.S. and non-U.S. equity and debt is artificial from any economic perspective. Realistically, simple tax code changes can cause shifts in debt and equity issuance that do not affect total net new issuance. These shifts merely reflect economic responses to changes in the tax-induced incentive structure. Despite the discussion of equity and debt issuance, the most important consideration is aggregate net new issuance and the combination of this aggregate number with cash income.

Estimating net new issuance is made difficult by the complexity of data in the United States and the paucity of data abroad. U.S. data are available from the Federal Reserve flow-of-funds statistics. Figure 30 shows historical U.S. net new equity issuance from 1953 through 1994. The 1980s merger and acquisition wave stands out as negative rates of issuance, because most deals were debt-for-stock transactions. In other words, the years from 1984 to 1990 were characterized by a shrinkage in outstanding equity attributable, in part, to the merger-induced reduction of common stock outstanding. Another period of corporate combinations began in 1994, as re-engineering and cost containment changed the corporate landscape and strategic rather than hostile acquisitions became popular. These deals are primarily stock-for-stock deals and do not result in net new issuance. We consider the 1980s to be aberrant and expect net equity issuance in the future to hover around the long-term rate of 0.5 percent.

---

[29]This difficulty arises from the fact that we are presenting a general equilibrium model in a sequential rather than simultaneous manner.

Figure 30. Net New Equity Issuance: United States, 1953–94

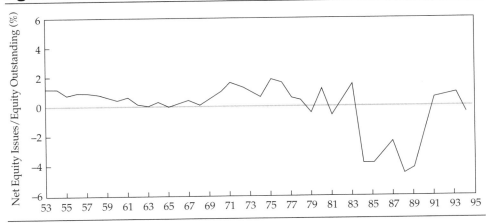

Figure 31 shows historical U.S. net new debt issuance. Net new issuance of debt surged in the late 1960s and 1970s on the back of expanding federal government debt and in the 1980s with the combined growth of federal, state, and local debt. The federal debt growth rate peaked in about 1980 and declined into the mid-1990s. Corporate debt shows a pattern that mirrors that of equity net new issuance, surging in 1984 and remaining relatively high through the period of aggressive debt-for-equity corporate acquisitions.

Conflicting developments are likely in the near future. Increased corporate merger activity may boost total debt new issuance, but because the current acquisition wave is dominated by strategic stock-for-stock deals, the impact on total issuance is likely to be minimal. The United States, however, as well as the rest of the world, appears poised to embark upon a period of reduced government borrowing activity. Consequently, the historical data measure a period of relatively high debt issuance. In the future, total U.S. debt net new issuance is likely to vary around the 4 percent level.

Non-U.S. net new issuance data are hard to obtain. A useful heuristic provides acceptable estimates of historical net new issuance. For equity assets, net new issuance can be estimated as the smoothed change in market capitalization less the price appreciation of the market. Price appreciation is used rather than total return because dividends represent a cash payment.

Figure 31. Net New Debt Issuance: United States, 1953–94

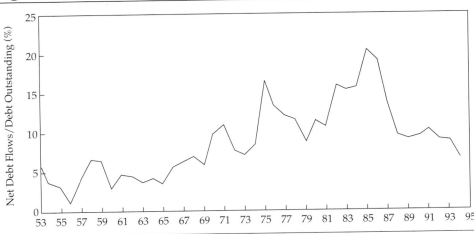

We tested the efficacy of this proxy for net new issuance by comparing the proxy-implied net new equity issuance in the United States with the more exact measure derived from the flow-of-funds data. Figure 32 illustrates this comparison. The estimated measure is more volatile than the measure based on flow-of-funds data, but it indicates the same general rate of net new issuance.

Figure 32. Actual and Estimated Net New Equity Issuance: United States, 1953–94

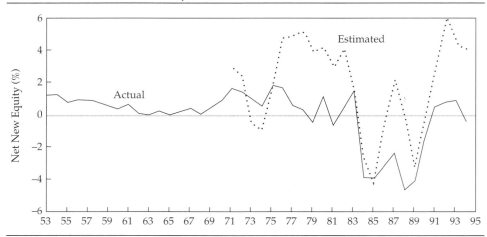

Applying this measure to non-U.S. markets (a subset of which is shown in Figure 33) indicates that net new equity issuance has ranged roughly between 0 and 5 percent. Non-U.S. net new equity issuance is expected to be about 5 percent. In the intermediate term, equity issuance is likely to remain on the high side as privatizations unwind the nationalizations that took place in the 1970s.

A proxy based on available data was also used for non-U.S. bond net new issuance. The proxy was tested for the United States against the more accurate flow-of-funds

Figure 33. Net New Equity Issuance: Canada, France, Germany, Japan, and United Kingdom, 1970–96

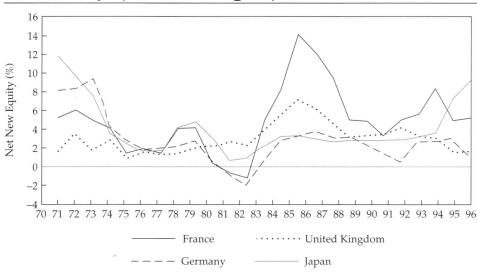

estimate. Figure 34 demonstrates that the percentage change in U.S. gross federal debt and the ratio of the U.S. deficit to total U.S. debt provide effective proxies for the true level of net new debt issuance.

Figure 35 shows the change in gross federal debt for Germany, Japan, and the United Kingdom from 1970 to 1996. Based on analysis of gross federal debt and deficit levels across the full range of non-U.S. countries, the estimated rate of net new issuance of non-U.S. debt is 7.0 percent.

Each of these net new issuance estimates was country weighted in order to derive the world total, shown in Table 3. Based on the bottom-up combination of individual estimates, the future rate of global equity issuance is expected to be 3.1 percent, and the U.S. rate should be substantially below that of non-U.S. markets. The rate of global debt issuance is substantially above that of equities, at 5.6 percent. Again, the U.S. rate is below the non-U.S. rate. The total net new issuance of the world is expected to be 4.8 percent.

Figure 34. Estimates of Net New Debt Issuance: United States, 1953–96

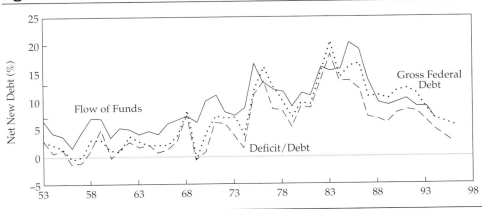

Figure 35. Estimates of Net New Debt Issuance: Germany, Japan, and United Kingdom, 1971–96

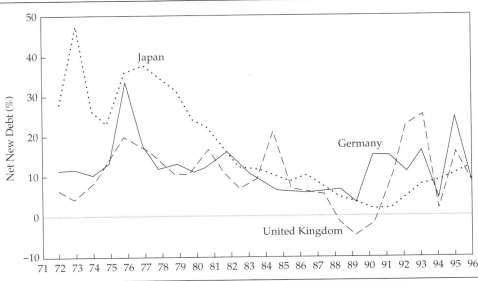

Table 3. Net New Issuance of Debt and Equity

Region	Net New Issuance
Equity	
United States	0.5%
Non-U.S.	5.0
Global	3.1
Debt	
United States	4.0
Non-U.S.	7.0
Global	5.6
World total	4.8

The preceding discussion has provided a systematic approach to estimating the components of the aggregate real global capital market return. The forward-looking real growth rate is estimated to be 4.0 percent. The net cash flow of the aggregate global capital market is equal to income less decrements to this income stream in the form of net new issuance. Income is estimated to be 4.9 percent and net new issuance 4.8 percent. The aggregate real return formula,

$$R_r = \left[\left(\frac{I_K}{W_K}\right) - \left(\frac{N_1}{W_K}\right)\right] + G_r,$$

provides an estimate of the real return to global capital markets in a fully integrated environment—4.1 percent ([4.9 percent – 4.8 percent] + 4.0 percent = 4.1 percent). The return, R_r, is the real pretax capital market return that is expected to be provided by all claims on global financial assets. The risk premium afforded global capital markets is determined by subtracting the real risk-free rate from the real return. Because the real risk-free rate is estimated to be 2.0 percent, the expected long-term global capital market risk premium is 2.1 percent.

Global Capital Market Risk. To compute the price of risk (the risk premium per unit of risk), one needs an estimate of the risk of the global capital market. As a starting point, observing and understanding the volatility pattern of a historical global capital market index is useful. To construct such an index, we used the definitions of and values for the claims on assets described in Chapter 2. On December 31, 1995, the equity and fixed-income portions of global market capitalization, detailed in Figure 36, amounted to $37,570.7 billion in the aggregate. This portfolio is much more broadly defined than those of most investors; it cuts across not only different countries but also different asset classes. With market value weighting, the portfolio is composed of slightly more than one-third equity markets and less than two-thirds bond markets. A good deal of the seemingly "oversized" debt share is attributable to the fondness of governments for deficit financing during the 1980s.

Figure 37 traces three intertemporal measures of global capital market volatility from 1970 to 1997. The rolling five-year measure is the standard deviation over time of a moving 60-month period of equally weighted, continuously compounded returns. The exponential measure is the standard deviation over time, in which the most recent period's squared deviation is given the greatest weight and prior squared deviations have declining weights going back in time. The visual advantage of exponential standard deviations is that they do not demonstrate the plateaus that arise in rolling standard deviations because of single events. GARCH (generalized autoregressive conditional heteroscedasticity) volatilities are based on the long-term volatility, the

Figure 36. Global Market Capitalization

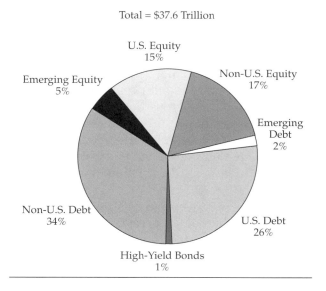

Total = $37.6 Trillion

U.S. Equity
15%

Emerging Equity
5%

Non-U.S. Equity
17%

Emerging
Debt
2%

Non-U.S. Debt
34%

U.S. Debt
26%

High-Yield Bonds
1%

Figure 37. Standard Deviations for the Global Investable Market, 1970–96

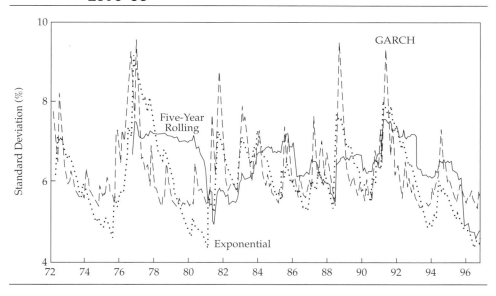

prior period's volatility forecast, and the difference between the prior period's expected and actual return. This approach makes sense if current volatility estimates are based on adjusting long-term volatility in response to recent volatility and what was learned in the latest period. GARCH has the advantage of providing a long-term, unconditional volatility estimate. The exponential and GARCH volatility estimates are similar, in that they reflect the observed phenomenon of volatility clustering, in which high-volatility and low-volatility periods appear in clusters.

Figure 37 suggests that the annualized standard deviation of monthly global capital market returns has varied around a rather stable level of 6.25 percent. The unconditional GARCH estimate for annualized global capital market monthly return volatility is 6.30 percent.

Monthly volatilities may not be the most appropriate measure of historical global capital market risk. If the market's investment horizon is longer than one month, then we will want to look at volatilities for longer intervals than one month. Over the range of frequencies from 1 month to 12 months, historical risk measures of 7–8 percent seem reasonable.

Central bank independence and more-stable inflation rates are likely in the future to reduce the uncertainty associated with real capital market cash flows. Also, the freedom with which capital flows across borders is likely to reduce the abilities of fiscal and monetary authorities to pursue variable and unconsidered policies.

The period since 1969 has been relatively benign for capital markets. Although the market was witness to two oil shocks and thoughtless fiscal and monetary policies, it did not experience the large-scale destruction of wealth that can arise from events such as war.[30]

Based on these influences, as well as other qualitative considerations, we forecast a global capital market volatility of 7.0 percent. This estimate can be interpreted as the uncertainty around the expected long-term global capital market return. The expected return is the sum of the real risk-free rate of 2.0 percent, the inflation premium of 2.1 percent, and the risk premium of 2.1 percent, or 7.0 percent in all. The expected return thus has a range of roughly –7.0 percent to +21.0 percent (plus and minus two standard deviations).

Price of Risk. The price of risk is the global capital market Sharpe ratio—the risk premium required per unit of risk incurred. Based on the expected long-term global capital market risk premium of 2.1 percent, an investment horizon of roughly six months, and an estimated annualized risk of 7.0 percent over the investment horizon, the price of risk is 2.1 percent divided by 7.0 percent, or about 0.30 percent. To determine the risk premium of individual asset classes, markets, and assets, we thus assumed a price of 0.30 percent.

In accordance with the Capital Market Line, risk tolerance differences among investors do not require the assumption of different prices of risk. In equilibrium, investors accommodate risk tolerance differences by combining the market portfolio with lending or borrowing in order to satisfy risk preferences. We made the assumption that all investors demand the same price of risk from all risky assets; in other words, the compensation required is independent of the source of risk.

Distribution of Market Risk Premium among Assets

Different risks associated with various assets result in different risk premiums for the assets. If capital markets provide an expected aggregate risk premium of 2.1 percent, then the weighted average of the expected long-term risk premiums of all component assets must equal 2.1 percent. As long as capital markets are fully integrated and adhere to the posited assumptions, the risk premiums for all individual assets can be determined by applying the multicurrency CAPM.

Recall from Equation 25 that the risk premium of an asset is based on the correlation of that asset's risk premium with the market's risk premium, the risk, and the price of risk.

Table 4 shows historical data for the risk premiums of the Canadian, German, Japanese, U.K., and U.S. equity and debt markets. The U.S. equity market is represented

---

[30]Brown, Goetzmann, and Ross (1995) argue that even the long-term returns that people are accustomed to evaluating for the U.S. and U.K. markets are not representative, because those markets survived periods of extreme turbulence. Not all markets have been so lucky, and therefore, these two markets provide a biased window into historical risk.

Table 4. Historical Risk Premiums and Components, December 31, 1969–September 30, 1996

Market/Country	Single-Asset Markets			Global Market		
	Implied $(r_i - c_i)$	ρ_{im}	σ_i	Price of Risk	$r_m - c_m$	σ_m
				0.36	2.3%	6.4%
Equity						
Canada	4.3%	0.70	17.0%			
Germany	3.4	0.52	17.7			
Japan	3.7	0.54	18.8			
United Kingdom	5.2	0.68	21.4			
United States	4.9	0.86	15.8			
Bond						
Canada	1.4	0.54	7.0			
Germany	0.6	0.44	3.9			
Japan	0.5	0.35	4.2			
United Kingdom	1.1	0.37	8.3			
United States	1.3	0.61	6.0			

by the Wilshire 5000 Index, and the U.S. bond market by the Salomon Brothers Broad Investment Grade (BIG) Bond Index. Data for the non-U.S. equity markets are derived using the Morgan Stanley Capital International indexes, and data for the non-U.S. bond markets are from the Salomon Brothers Government Bond indexes. All standard deviation and correlation computations are based on annualized monthly data. The implied risk premium is computed based on the historical global capital market price of risk of 0.36 and each market's correlation and standard deviation.

Rather than using historical data, we drew upon the aggregate economic framework and the derived capital market price of risk. By applying this price of risk to equilibrium risk and correlation estimates for each market, we could compute equilibrium asset-class risk premiums. Just as we estimated the future volatility of the global capital market, we also estimated equity and bond market risks.

Historical risk premium volatilities provide a useful starting point. Figure 38 shows the annualized monthly risk premium standard deviations on a rolling five-year, exponential, and GARCH basis for five countries' equity and bond markets. Among the equity markets, it is difficult if not impossible to discern any volatility trend over time. Recent research has documented the tendency of volatilities to cluster for high-frequency daily data, but this tendency has been more difficult to prove for lower frequency data, such as monthly or quarterly returns. Events such as the oil price shocks in the 1970s and the 1987 market decline are evident in many of the data series.

The bond markets have exhibited a distinct decline in volatilities since the money supply and credit volatility of the late 1970s and early 1980s, brought on by the August 1971 suspension of the Bretton Woods worldwide system of maintaining fixed exchange rates linked to a gold standard.[31] Absent this unique period, bond volatilities have been stable, and we expect them to decline in the future. The correlation of central bank independence with the volatility of inflation is –0.74. Increasing central bank independence and declining inflation volatilities should put downward pressure on bond volatilities and ultimately on bond risk premiums.

---

[31]The analysis of markets has been simplified for the purposes of this discussion. Rather than an evaluation of overall bond market volatility, a more accurate analysis would be based on yield volatility and market structure. Likewise, an analysis of equity markets that takes into account considerations such as industry composition, leverage, and other factors would be more accurate. In effect, for the sake of exposition, we took a simplified top-down approach, although a bottom-up approach would be much more effective.

Figure 38. Standard Deviations for the Equity and Bond Markets: Canada, Germany, Japan, United Kingdom, and United States, 1970–96

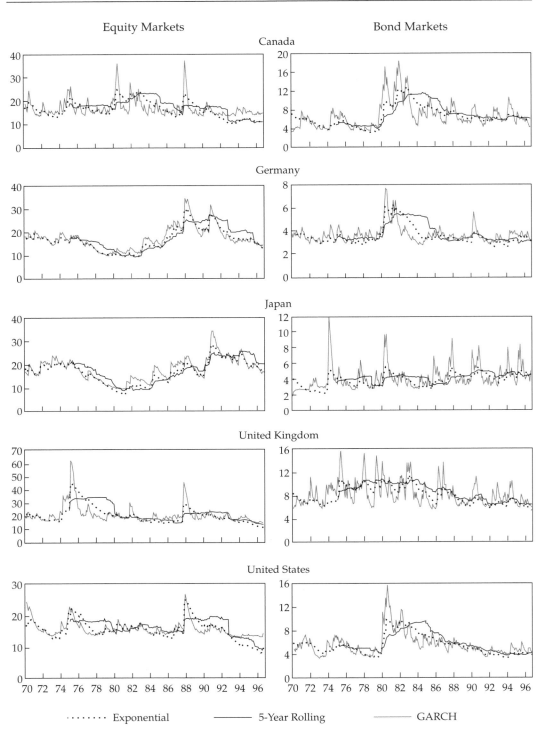

Note: Standard deviations are in percentages.

Analysis of historical equity data again provides a useful departure point for estimating future equilibrium correlations of each market with the global capital market, which are shown in Figure 39. Even though the global capital market is dominated by fixed-income assets, equity markets are more volatile than debt markets, thereby dominating the volatility of the global capital market index and resulting in equity market correlations that are at or above those of debt markets.

Bond and equity market correlations with the global capital market tend to increase as the frequency of measuring returns declines. Focusing on frequencies ranging from 1 to 12 months tends to suggest historical correlations over the assumed market investment horizon that are higher than the monthly return correlations.

Table 5 combines all aspects of the price of risk, volatility, and correlation analysis to identify estimates of the equilibrium risk premiums of the equity and bond markets in the five countries in our analysis. The estimates in the left-hand columns of the table are based on a fully integrated global framework in which individual markets compensate for systematic risk with respect to the global capital market.

Table 5. Long-Term Fully Integrated and Fully Segmented Expected Risk Premiums

Market/Country	Fully Integrated			Fully Segmented	
	$(r_i - c_i)$	ρ_{im}	σ_i	$(r_i - c_i)$	σ_I
Equity					
Canada	3.4%	0.70	16.0%	4.8%	16.0%
Germany	3.3	0.60	18.5	5.6	18.5
Japan	3.6	0.60	20.0	6.0	20.0
United Kingdom	3.9	0.75	17.5	5.3	17.5
United States	4.0	0.85	15.8	4.7	15.8
Bond					
Canada	1.2	0.65	6.2	1.9	6.2
Germany	0.7	0.60	3.7	1.1	3.7
Japan	0.9	0.55	5.7	1.7	5.7
United Kingdom	1.2	0.55	7.0	2.1	7.0
United States	1.1	0.75	4.7	1.4	4.7

Despite the fact that global markets for goods, services, and assets are not fully integrated, consideration of the globally integrated case is valuable. The fully integrated case is a lower limit both for systematic risk and for equilibrium risk premiums.

The capital markets are inexorably, albeit slowly, moving toward global integration. In an environment in which markets are not fully integrated, the risk premium for an individual asset would be determined by a subset of all investors. Generally, these investors would command a relatively high risk premium for that asset because of its relatively large portion in their portfolios and, therefore, its high perceived systematic risk. All investors not in that subset would perceive a risk premium on that asset that is relatively high; the asset would afford substantial diversification relative to the risk premium available. Investors would thus be presented every day with the incentive to find legal, as well as illegal, avenues around market regulations and inhibitions to capture these advantageous risk premiums. Over time, capital would move in a manner consistent with increasing global integration.

The other end of the spectrum is the fully segmented case. If capital markets were fully segmented, then the risk premium of each market would be set in isolation,

Figure 39. Correlations of Equity and Bond Markets with Global Capital Market: Canada, Germany, Japan, United Kingdom, and United States, 1970–96

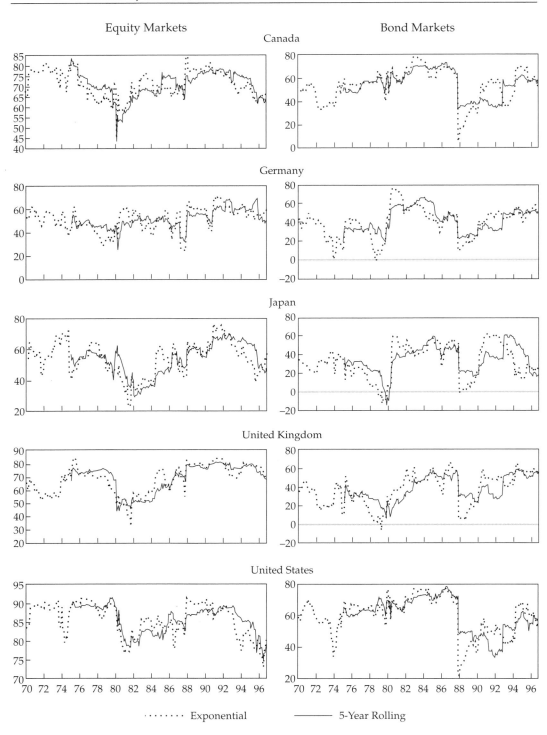

Note: Correlations are in percentages.

Table 6. Long-Term Fully Home-Biased and Regional Expected Risk Premiums

Market/Country	Home Biased			Regional		
	$(r_i - c_i)$	ρ_{im}	σ_i	$(r_i - c_i)$	ρ_{im}	σ_I
Equity						
Canada	5.4%	0.95	15.50%	4.3%	0.75	15.50%
Germany	5.6	0.80	19.00	4.6	0.65	19.00
Japan	6.6	0.85	21.00	6.6	0.85	21.00
United Kingdom	7.0	0.99	19.00	6.3	0.90	19.00
United States	5.7	0.97	16.00	5.6	0.95	16.00
Bond						
Canada	1.4	0.60	6.50	1.1	0.45	6.50
Germany	1.2	0.80	4.00	0.9	0.60	4.00
Japan	1.0	0.60	4.75	1.1	0.60	4.75
United Kingdom	1.5	0.55	7.75	1.7	0.60	7.75
United States	1.2	0.55	6.00	1.2	0.55	6.00

reflecting the risk of the asset without regard to its diversification potential.[32] The fully segmented risk premium of each market, presented in the right-hand columns of Table 5, is the price of risk times its segmented volatility. We still assume the price of risk to be invariant to the investor and the degree of segmentation. The fully segmented risk premiums should serve as an upper bound for systematic risk and equilibrium risk premiums. To the extent that capital flows across borders and investors increasingly hold varying degrees of globally diversified portfolios, an individual asset or even a market is unlikely to be priced in isolation.

Between the bounds established by fully integrated and segmented analysis is a broad range of possible risk premiums for each market. Within this range, the typical portfolio allocation of an investor in each country was used to determine a more appropriate estimate of the market risk premium. Two typical portfolios were used to analyze this partially integrated analysis. The first makes use of InterSec Research Corporation's "Ownership of Assets" survey. The allocation grids, generated annually by InterSec, enable identification of typical portfolio holdings of investors in each country. The data are categorized as cash equivalents, domestic bonds, domestic equity, foreign bonds, foreign equity, loans and mortgages, real estate, and other. The most noteworthy aspect of the data is the propensity of investors to hold domestic assets—we refer to this tendency as "home bias." The foreign component of this case is considered to be a market-capitalization-weighted allocation across markets.

The second case of partial integration uses the same InterSec portfolio allocation data but assumes that the foreign portfolio holdings are regional in nature. This assumption incorporates the growing importance of regional blocs, such as the European Monetary Union. We refer to this case as the regional case.

Table 6 lists the risk premiums that would be implied by the two partially integrated cases. These premiums reflect varying assumptions with regard to partial integration. The risk premiums generally lie between the fully integrated and segmented cases, providing an indication of the systematic risks and risk premiums that each equity and bond market is likely to be pricing today.[33]

---

[32]Actually, the broad market could be considered the individual country market itself, and the correlation would be 1.

[33]The U.S. risk premium from the home-biased analysis and the U.S. and Canadian risk premiums from the regional analysis fall below their respective fully integrated risk premiums. We attribute this finding to the home-biased and regional portfolio allocations that are based on surveys of a subset of the investing population.

The final set of equilibrium risk premiums used for asset, market, and asset class valuation depends on the degree of integration that is thought currently to exist and is anticipated to evolve during the coming decades. Also, purely quantitative measures of volatilities and risk premiums must be adjusted to account for qualitative considerations of relevance to the equilibrium pricing of assets. Final risks and risk premiums would be based on the quantitative projections in Tables 5 and 6 and consideration of qualitative factors, such as confidence in the quantitative projections themselves, liquidity, and political risk.

Conclusion

We have provided a theoretical framework for estimating equilibrium levels of the real risk-free rate, inflation premiums, and risk premiums based on a sound economic foundation. This framework could be used for any number of equilibrium estimates based on different assumptions. Although equilibrium can differ, this framework provides a way of estimating macroeconomically consistent returns across all markets and asset classes.

If all of the analysis had been purely quantitative under the assumption of full integration, then an optimization would have yielded the global capital market as an efficient portfolio. Because we interjected qualitative considerations and assumed an environment of partial integration, we would not expect the global capital market to lie on the efficient frontier. Consequently, policy allocations derived from optimizations based on equilibrium return estimates will deviate from the global capital market allocation.

References

Alesina, Alberto, and Lawrence H. Summers. 1993. "Central Bank Independence and Macroeconomic Performance." *Journal of Money, Credit, and Banking*, vol. 25, no. 2 (May):151–62.

Brown, Stephen, William Goetzmann, and Stephen Ross. 1995. "Survival." *Journal of Finance*, vol. 50, no. 3 (July):853–73.

Diermeier, Jeffrey J. 1990. "Capital Market Expectations: The Macro Factors." In *Managing Investment Portfolios: A Dynamic Process,* 2nd ed., edited by John L. Maginn and Donald L. Tuttle. New York: Warren Gorham & Lamont:5-1–5-77.

Diermeier, Jeffrey J., Roger G. Ibbotson, and Laurence B. Siegel. 1984. "The Supply of Capital Market Returns." *Financial Analysts Journal*, vol. 40, no. 2 (March/April): 74–80.

Gordon, Myron, and E. Shapiro. 1956. "Capital Equipment Analysis: The Required Rate of Profit." *Management Science*, vol. 3 (October): 102–10.

Griliches, Zvi. 1994. "Productivity, R&D, and the Data Constraint." *American Economic Review*, vol. 84 (March):1–23.

Karnosky, Denis S., and Brian D. Singer. 1994. *Global Asset Management and Performance Attribution.* Charlottesville VA: Research Foundation of the Institute of Chartered Financial Analysts.

Modigliani, Franco, and Merton H. Miller. 1958. "The Cost of Capital, Corporation Finance and the Theory of Investment." *American Economic Review*, vol. 48 (June):261–97.

Reilly, Frank K., and Rashida A. Akhtar. 1995. "The Benchmark Error Problem with Global Capital Markets." *Journal of Portfolio Management*, vol. 22, no. 1 (Fall):33–52.

Reilly, Frank K., and Keith Brown. 1997. *Investment Analysis and Portfolio Management*, 4th ed. New York: Dryden Press.

Sharpe, William F. 1963. "A Simplified Model of Portfolio Analysis." *Management Science*, vol. 7 (January):277–93.

Tobin, James. 1958. "Liquidity Preference as Behavior toward Risk." *Review of Economic Studies*, vol. 25, no. 2 (February):65–85.

Selected AIMR Publications

AIMR Performance Presentation Standards Handbook, 2nd edition, 1996

Deregulation of the Electric Utility Industry, 1997

Economic Analysis for Investment Professionals, 1997

Finding Reality in Reported Earnings, 1997
Jan R. Squires, CFA, *Editor*

Global Equity Investing, 1996

Global Portfolio Management, 1996
Jan R. Squires, CFA, *Editor*

Implementing Global Equity Strategy: Spotlight on Asia, 1997

Investing in Small-Cap and Microcap Securities, 1997

Managing Endowment and Foundation Funds, 1996

Managing Investment Firms: People and Culture, 1996
Jan R. Squires, CFA, *Editor*

Merck & Company: A Comprehensive Equity Valuation Analysis, 1996
Randall S. Billingsley, CFA

Readings in Venture Capital, 1997

Risk Management, 1996

Standards of Practice Casebook, 1996

Standards of Practice Handbook, 7th edition, 1996

A full catalog of publications is available on AIMR's World Wide Web site at **www.aimr.org**; or you may write to AIMR, P.O. Box 3668, Charlottesville, VA 22903 U.S.A.; call 1-804-980-3668; fax 1-804-963-6826; or e-mail **info@aimr.org** to receive a free copy. All prices are subject to change.